THE BEST POEMS AND POETS OF 2004

The International Library of Poetry

Howard Ely, Editor

The Best Poems and Poets of 2004

Proudly manufactured in the United States of America by
Watermark Press
One Poetry Plaza
Owings Mills, MD 21117

poetry.COM
The International Library of Poetry

FOREWORD

Throughout life, we store information collected from experiences and try in some way to make sense of it. When we are not able to fully understand the things that occur in our lives, we often externalize the information. By doing this, we are afforded a different perspective, thus allowing us to think more clearly about difficult or perplexing events and emotions. Art is one of the ways in which people choose to externalize their thoughts.

Within the arts, modes of expression differ, but poetry is a very powerful tool by which people can share sometimes confusing, sometimes perfectly clear concepts and feelings with others. Intentions can run the gamut as well: The artists may simply want to share something that has touched their lives in some way, or they may want to get help to allay anxiety or uncertainty. The poetry within *The Best Poems and Poets of 2004* is from every point on the spectrum: every topic, every intention, every event or emotion imaginable. Some poems will speak to certain readers more than others, but it is always important to keep in mind that each verse is the voice of a poet, of a mind that needs to make sense of this world, of a heart that feels the effects of every moment in this life, and perhaps of a memory that is striving to surface. Nonetheless, recalling our yesterdays gives birth to our many forms of expression.

The Best Poems and Poets of 2004

Artist's Profile
Armin Wilson
Kennett Square, Pennsylvania, USA

I was born in Sapulpa, Oklahoma, a little town southeast of Tulsa. I'm eighty-seven, and have been writing poetry for fifty years. I'm a chemist by profession. I write objective/descriptive poetry about observations on the universe. In fifty years I've written one personal, limited autobiographic poem. First person singular poems hold no interest for me, probably because of my scientific training. I do, though, enjoy all kinds of poetry and read extensively in poetry and other fields. I'm Zen Buddhist, because Zen Buddhism is more than a little crazy and contradictory. It fits like a glove the world we inhabit. I was so sad about John Lennon, for whom I wrote this poem. The world lost a unique, irreplaceable figure!

Leaving the Shore

The key that unlocks the earth
He knew
Held it in his hand
Then after he gave us all in happiness,
Understanding, beauty, grandeur
(You know the song, so philosophical)
Felled by the bullet of the assassin
Felled by the corrupt mind that
Sits grinning in all of us
Being human, being imperfect
We all held the gun

Our sacrifice to the gods
Seeking to stave off evil
And gaining the inevitable

Yes
When will we ever learn to
Not crush the flowers
That emblematic something
Yet
Learn we must

Mother Nature,
Please call home

Armin Wilson

Lengthening Shadows

There was a time
When the shoulders of the hills shrugged
The halo-topped trees into
The browning river
The sun played hide-and-seek
With our phantasmagoric fingers
As we tried to grab its hand
Never were we so close
Time knew us not in our youth
Everything was aglow
Everything was aflame with light and
We stopped in wonder
Stopped to see the ebbing wind slowly fade away
While the dancing sun's grace-gilded feet
Swam west, long tired of play
They waved to us through
A receding sea of broken leaves
We reached a yearning arm
If but to only catch the time lost in the foam
But seeing mere remains (he had moved on)
We turned into the dark and made for home

Matt Sumpter

Amid the Sand

To Eva Fernandez, with love

Amid the sand that suffers so, from
heat and sun as I lie low within its
womb where nary live, but only
slowly die. I grasp its granules made
of glass as mind takes flight and
dreams of grass, and dewy leaves
that grace a field adorned with
bluest sky. In dimmest hopes I raise
my limbs up from the barren bed and
dunes, to songs that ring out well
within this heart that will not die.
The lyrics speak of things unknown,
yet undiscovered but surely sown,
and spring to life though I'm its
seed as my arms lift to rise. I
stare the sun down from its stead
that sears and beats upon my head,
bewildered as I sing to praise its
warming rays that come. No more
abused leathered skin and fallen
faith that once despaired, the sun
shines forth upon this bed where new
songs have begun.

Terry L. Spence

Listen

The wind tells a story in the suburbs
in full discourse
with tall, valiant trees.
It rolls, has space, momentum,
a flow no buildings interrupt;
disclosed on a sheer journey,
less is salvaged in the Bronx,
just anecdotes to designated trees.

Paul Camacho

Teenage Tension

You settled on my troubled chest,
a thin, cold veil trailing miles of years with clouds and showers,
the sun occasionally peeking through, casting a rare rainbow.

We were mother and daughter set in a single mold
of daily interaction.
You were not kind, caring, nor tolerant.
I vainly sought the thread,
the nettlesome aggravation of many grievances, now dead.

Your blue eyes danced with scintillating charm
to please your many friends.
I saw you from a distance, noting your resistance,
your vitality, your persistence with the cocoon spun
'round your private world.

Through blurred eyes I recalled the patient love of mothers
"enduring all things, hoping all things."

Perhaps, perhaps the distance music will resonate
and strike a note of mutual accord.

Jane Peters

Dangerous Melancholy

To David J., I love you madly

There will be no encore
of wistful musing.
I have begun writing postcards
to myself,
recalling wine
I did not drink in Florence,
candles burning languid
dangerously low
in a Paris cafe,
those ruffles of silver leaves
cluttering the path
to the house I forgot to live in.
I gave myself a bouquet of clouds
the day I said,
"Forget my birthday,"
but you arrived at midnight
with white rain-soaked lilies
on the verge of blooming,
when violets would have been enough.

Mara Squar

El Salvador

To my mama, who came to the U.S. in 1939

Thick foliage envelopes
the crowded nation.
Men, women, and children stream
like rushing rivers
on highways and pathways
in an abused land.
Poverty abounds
while those more fortunate
live in fortresses
shielded from the misery
that thrives outside their walls.
El Salvador . . .
screaming a muzzled cry,
her beauty shrouded in suffering
dealt by the powerful
who cover their ears
so as not to hear.
Their gun is greed . . .
the victims,
the poor who struggle
for life
in a tiny and crippled land.

Laurina Marnie Kusell

Shopping

Together we buy wallpaper
To cover the cracks in our marriage,
Heavy-duty paste
To hold together a broken relationship.

A warm orange duvet
For a bed that has grown cold,
Coordinating curtains to pull over
And shut out the truth.

We take great care,
Ensuring everything matches,
That we're not paying too high a price.
Unfortunately, we don't, and we did.

Linda Collins

Letting Go

My body is a wild tambourine,
wire-whipped by wind,
shelled by engine sounds.

I hold my breath and leap;
the chute opens like a panther slug on my back
and swings me,
an unwinding puppet, high
above green-sectioned landscape.

Gliding silently down, I notice
my untied shoelace.

Gillian McConnell

Artist's Profile
Catherine Chandler
Beaconsfield, QC, Canada

I am an American formalist poet currently living and working in Canada. My poems and translations have been widely published, or will soon appear, in such literary journals as "SPSM&H," "The Lyric," "Iambs and Trochees," "The Dark Horse," "Harp-Strings Poetry Journal," "Raintown Review," "Blue Unicorn," and others.

Elderberry

In honor of my grandmother, Estelle Smith

When I was twelve, a gangling freckled sprout
without specific plans to fill my day,
I went offhand to Granny's house. No doubt
I'd hear (again) of olden times, the way
each day was given to a different chore.
Her aged, knotted hands bore out the word;
for years they'd wrung the wash, they'd scrubbed the floor,
they'd kneaded, knitted, nursed. But as she stirred
the pungent crimson juice whose droplets wept
through cheesecloth to a saucepan on the stove,
I failed to measure promises she'd kept,
and thought the Mason jars defined her love.
Now that I understand, I ache to taste
those sweet provisions, once consumed in haste.

Catherine Chandler

Joelle of the Star-Spray

You are as primitive phosphorus enfleshed, cinnamon's fey sister.
Sublime, you flow with fire as a force of light;
Luminous, you burn with curves as the earth of summer
As your form becomes everything wild and electric.

Open your eyes, and hazelnuts flower full of emeralds.
Sigh a moment, and hot moon moisture ignites ethereal.
You are the essence of humid earth fruit oceans
When their embrace mirages together foaming pearl.

O' summer meteor, let me caress your heart of dusk.
Let me caress your saffron soft halos glimmering from within
Through the innocent fondling of the eye
And see how soft topaz honey suffuses as your skin.

Let me caress the amber silkscapes suffusing your divine heat
Through the pure incandescence of touch
And encompass their intimate turbulence where meet
The glistening wet gleaming cream brightful moons.

You are vision who pierces the veils of sight:
The first light that pierces the sky foams,
The last clouds that become the sea of flight,
And echo there the memory of the Earth of butterflies.

Ernest L. Davis

The Resurrection
Dawn on Yano

This morning I awoke in dew,
enshrouded by the ghosts of rain
wanting to come back again,
while in the east, the hills and trees
I swear were bursting into flames.
I rose slowly,
quiet,
looking.

Frank Simpleton

Smoker's Cough

Inhale the smoke, blur, my innermost confusion;
Exhale the fumes, but the burning remains.
Smell the beautiful aroma as if it's you.
Part of you.
Just this part of you remains. You . . .
Smoke, mixed with cologne, mixed with
Leather . . .
Mixed with passion, swirls of uncertainty, tinges of doubt.
My mouth curls round the cigarette, fingertips brush my lips.
I close my eyes and smell you in layers.
Smell you, feel you, taste you . . .
Until only ash is left.
Flicking the cigarette to the ground,
Rolling it beneath my heel.
I walk past it,
But
Look back
And notice its last deadly flames that refuse to be quenched.

Michelle Kroop

Water Lilies
To my family

Blooming, only the night sky comes
close to the sight of the water lily.
White flowers grace
peaceful wetness.
The wind whispers secrets
for only nature's beauties to hear.
Their namesake is their final place
for a home.
Colorful flowers and green-skinned creatures call lilypads home.
Water lilies satisfy the need for
nature's pleasantness.

Kelly Frank

Artist's Profile
Sally McLean
Mornington, Australia

I began my love of the written word in my teenage years, going on to become a published poet at the age of fifteen, which continues to the present day. I have been published in various anthologies in Australia, the UK, the U.S., and Canada. I branched out to short stories and children's tales in 2000, again being published in magazines and anthologies in Australia, the UK, the U.S., and Canada. My latest guise is that of a screenwriter, with two feature film scripts sold to companies in the UK and Australia, and a third under development.

Undercover

For my inspiration and best friend, my mother, Marg

The cries of the gulls
as they swoop and soar
across the flat wooden slats
of the pier,
ducking, diving, dodging
as the girl stares
wondering
at the vista before her.
Do you see the scars,
the gashes of life
that run across her soul
once covered by a plastered smile?
A rosy, painted smile.
Under the cover of day
she watches . . . wishes . . . wonders
where is her childhood now?
Years have passed,
leaving their mark,
moving onto the next,
altering, amending, amplifying
her age anew.
Yet beneath the wrinkled exterior
beats the heart of the girl
who wonders.

Sally McLean

Do You Know Who Took Tomorrow?

It is the four-walled silence
that drowns out thought.
Left with the stale taste of cigarette smoke-clouded dream
of this separate living.
To sleep this oranged-purple day away
for want of the familiar song.
It all beats upon the brow
moist-wrinkled furrows, pensive
on the quantities of every action
and each separate word.
Walk the steps of the weary,
measured heavy-paced,
bearing more weight and time.
And the cries wail from the
eyeless children who seek the darkness of the morning,
when all the games will die
and wondering remains the
passion playground of mind's void.
And do you know who took tomorrow?
I had it in my back pocket . . .
and now it's gone.

Roger C. Sharpe

The Broken Curse

Encrusted in my island home that lies beyond the sea.
Still as my horizon grew, I sat in my wooden chair,
convinced I had ruined everything while through
the open window came the smell of sea breeze.
I sat quite still, my rosy scalp glistening
through my rather thin white hair.
On a day like any other day, like yesterday or centuries
before "my soul" in humble hope unscarred,
how gladly would I be a book
to your long pocket flaps.
I hung my verses in the wind,
time and tide their faults may find.
My brow is wet with honest sweat,
sweet antidote to sorrow, toil, and strife.
A shade of sadness, a blush of shame over my face
as a demon is hurled by an angel's spear,
heels over head, to his proper sphere.
So if I gulp my sorrows down, or see them drown,
in foamy draughts of old nut brown,
the melancholy days have come.

Patricia Ann Bratt

Skeleton Maze (Ode to the Minotaur)

And I feed,
Huddled in the center,
I hunger for revenge,
And drink in the bitter red Justice.
I laugh and gurgle to myself,
For as weak as these humans are,
I am but the shadow of a mistake,
A ghost in the closet.
I have been running,
Running in circles, of course.
Stink of sweat mingles with Death;
I am a clown trapped in the ring.
Salty tears dance with the crimson,
And I cannot help feeling alone,
Having never known love,
Never the embrace of happiness.
The quiet steps echo in the halls,
Reverberating and amplifying,
And I lie against the wall to wait,
Wait for another connection.

Chris Nag

Oceanside Jive

For childhood and Lincoln City dreams

She waddles like a penguin
back onto dry sand that awaits
the bucket of moisture and a buried father.
Is she crabbing?
Maybe laying foundation for a king's castle?
No.
Suddenly the bucket is poured,
downward and fierce upon Daddy's protesting cries.
Waves crash deceptively close,
thundering a cry of playfulness
that each soaks into their experiences.
The penguin girl communicates to Daddy by hand signals
of love and caution;
she is the deaf communicator of the hour,
controlling a sea of silent entertainment,
and I am the envious outsider,
taking notes on love and interaction.

Kelly E. Moylan

Life of the Morning Dew

As the sun rises on the eastern side
Shadows of western darkness hide
Cold wet dew clings with the dawn
In fields of grass where it's been drawn
As if caught now in the morning light
Giving reflections in silvery white
Letting loose of its staggering weight
Raising the blades and not too late
Stacking colors of bluish jade
Set out across an open glade
As water drops gather below
Resembling that of melting snow
Collecting now as in a well
Letting loose its grassy smell

Phillip Roberts

Cherry Blossoms

In loving memory of my grandma, Elizabeth Tan

We came from all different parts of the world
in huge flocks to see the cherry blossoms.
It's springtime now, they are all in full bloom.
Pretty in pink, oh, what a sight—behold!
'Tis true their beauty truly overwhelms.
Three days later, it was a shocking sight.
They have now all been strewn over the ground.
Suggestion and perishability,
the twin themes deep-rooted in human life.
The fall of the cherry blossoms suggest
the once-full bloom of new buds yet to come.
This subtle hint at life's impermanence.
Like the cherry blossoms, we'll die one day,
but unlike them, we really don't know when.

Lionel Lim

Sweet September
To Irina

The images astounded and confused me that day
As we watched the surreal drama unfold far away
A monumental accident, only that could it be
That instant transformation of the city by the sea
Your country, you asked, as the drama was shown
That day we first met, and our hearts were known
Our bond was intense, as you shared national pain
Walking in sorrow, through sunshine and rain
The embassy covered in flowers and small light
Foreigners became friends throughout the night
With bittersweet memories, this story is told
Of pain, yet sweetness, as new life would unfold
You, my sweet darling, through ensuing months and years,
Have shown me your love, born on a day of great tears
September for many, and count me as one,
Memories of sorrow, and a day with no sun
Yet through it all, I see sweet September
For we met that day, how sweet I remember

Larry Reed

Limited Life

To a true teacher, Mrs. Davina Ruben

Far beyond her realm of reality
She held her breath for happiness
Rubbing her eyes raw of her tears
And smoking her eighth cigarette in a row
She rips at her flesh to mentally maintain her living state
Paranoid by her own self-inflicted chaos
She will allow nothing to calm her storm
The rain hits the pavement like stones
Loud and fast they consume her dry clothes
With her maple-colored hair now but the wool over her eyes
A decision is to be made
Aching in her body is the soul she thought she lost
Not moving from her curb of contempt
A truck rolls slowly by her beckoning to move on
She struggles with the choice but remains in her position
Finding the strength or pride to create energy of resilience
She can't help but feel overwhelmed
This little life hasn't yet lived
But it's so afraid to give continue forward

Nicole Elysia Lopez

Deceit

Dedicated to blind love

I am a jaundiced coquette, limping
through varnished days, unmindful of
the twisted trellis suspended in
free play. I hiss as a numb
undercurrent of logic sends
hysterical vibrations up and down my
maudlin spine. But blood and thunder
can't penetrate the melodrama that
is entombed in my existential
vacuum. You see, my swarthy smirk
devours all mythological immortals
and my treacherous heart beguiles
with a Machiavellian illusion as it
whispers sweet nothings like a
charismatic vampire. But beware, for
I'll woo you with secret Siren songs
as I am an insincere seductress . . .
a designing provocateur perched high
on my lofty subterfuge, observing
the masquerade. Yes, I'm what you
call deceit. My masque is charm.
Fallacy sits at my right side;
Truth is my devil.

Bonny Deflandre

Hand Out

Grime-bejeweled, she smears her face,
fingers gnarled, clenching a napkin
left over from her last meal.

Eyes too heavy to lift
peer out with pregnant questing.
Brainstorms still as lightning,
quick words
force themselves:
"Spare change?"

The plane shared between two worlds,
small and ever moving,
permits no common ground of understanding.

We pass the moment and then
each other,
orbits without collision.

David Atkins

Artist's Profile
Benjamin Frazier
Alberta, VA, USA

I'm a college student at James Madison University. My goal is to change the world with my art. My main focus is film, and I plan on making documentaries and films based on true stories. I believe this world is in need of a revolution of the mind and soul. I'm going to do my part.

Beautiful Winter

To the lady in my dreams

Ice fingers dance across my face
She's filled with swirling leaves of grace
An ocean of warmth underneath my skin
My chest aches to hold your chin
I welcome the blue lady with a smile
I ask you to stay a little while
Your pulse echoes in my soul
Lady Winter charges her toll
Cold toes and cold fingers fill the day
During the night you wanna stay
I heat your flesh with my breath
And my loneliness dies its sweet death
Winter is beautiful

Benjamin Frazier

Artist's Profile

Sean M. York

Ponca City, OK, USA

This poem is the embodiment of my relationship with a woman whom I never should have loved, but did. We spent several wonderful weeks together, only to realize our mistake, and now we torture each other with forbidden romance.

Misguided Midnights
To Bernadette Stiles

Enchantment, endearment enthralled in your enticing face,
I slyly, slowly press my lips to yours.
Calmly and cooly, hold me closely,
Sway me smoothly; love me truly.
Wait, but stop, this is wrong.
Forbidden rendezvous in the silent night,
Unsteady lullabies won't make it right.
Let me go; no, stay instead,
I can't sleep with you in my head.
Hold me close and hold me tight,
For this might be our only night.
Loved you then, and love you still,
And perhaps you'll see I always will.
We've got our wrongs, and weighed the rights,
We'll always have these misguided midnights.

Sean M. York

This Murdered Clock

To birth and the history of legends

Sleep through the never red and always night,
the dye of ancient skins to twitch the tongue
and leave a citrus sting to blur your sight.
Such tears that mingle black . . . like film with lungs
that can't feed life into the dreaming well.
This pendulum constricts the wire-toothed time
and lingers with a copper, horrid smell . . .
your blood that dries like scabs of lemon-lime . . .
so that you're flown towards home, to eggshell yolks
of pulsing violinists, pastel tips
of petals cored with deepened purple strokes,
and moon so thick with liquid love and lips.
You taste your wings until the womb is ripe
for birth. You're thrust again into red life.

Amanda Guadayol

Whatever Happened to Lyric?

Whatever happened to lyric, the sun
leaving footprints across the sky,
opening arms to the embrace of love?
Whatever happened to lyric, lips
that pierce the deepest sorrow, a
voice that beams a gentle light,
which guides lost souls back to solid
rock? I ask, "Whatever happened to
lyric?" My lyric, my verse. Now I
have only melody, I have sound
without definition, just an empty
tune. Whatever happened to lyric, so
vibrant and strong, and then in the
blink of my eye, gone? I seek the
answers that give directions to where
my lyric lies. Until I find my lyric,
I'll sit in darkness as my soul
cries. I'll travel paths unknown
until my questions are answered and
there are no more whys.

Alvin O. Mitchell

Comforting Souls
For my children

I lost my mother today
In a crowd-filled hallway
When I turned for a moment
To look at a lady's strange hat.
I stood panic-stricken, trembling,
Until you broke through the throng
To gather me lovingly into your arms,
Comforting my six-year-old soul.
I lost my mother today
Amidst angry shouts, bitter tears,
Yelling "It's my life, not yours!"
I packed my bags, ready to leave,
To be free from your rule.
And with the infinite wisdom experience gives
You gathered me in your loving arms,
Comforting my warring, sixteen-year-old soul.
I lost my mother today.
The doctors called and said to come,
That your last moments were drawing near.
I held your hand, we both cried.
Where had all our time gone?
It seemed we'd finally become friends.
So I gathered you close this time in my loving arms,
Comforting your soul as you reluctantly let go.

Walanda Baker

Waiting for the Rain

Waiting for the rain
I smoke a cigarette
coiled on cold New England granite
twenty feet from where the man I married
lies molding among the weeds
of Potter's Field.
I had to jump three swollen streams
on the two-mile trail
to get here the back way,
though I could have climbed the hill
from the parking lot below.
Rotten beer cans and storm-sodden litter
tell me the kids from town do it all the time,
to party where no one hangs out.
But it's a Sunday afternoon and today
they're all at home
watching TV and doing homework
while I let the lichen dampen my pants
and the wind whips the smoke from my hand
to fling it into the trees.
My dog thinks I'm eating,
but declines a drag
and wanders off to chase chipmunks
through the cast-off crop of lowbush berries.

Betsy Jane Horne

untitled

lately i've been holding water,
hands cupped,
catching
the
droplets
as
they
fall.
like a goddess
in my curtained world,
queen
of a ceramic universe.
all alone
in my shower
i hold water.

Claire Staples

barren art

i am an anomaly
figure made for fond attentions
sparking interest near and far
responding well to male affection
wide hips to bear a dozen youth
of merry wit and sound transgression
but my womb will hold no life
from the art of my discretion
i'm doomed to live a carefree life
to counsel children not my own
this life will be my effigy
no blood will pass beyond my tomb
my children are of ink and type
brain children of the heart and mind
through them my stories live and shine
in them my prodigy you'll find

Elizabeth Gross

Artist's Profile
J. Joy Rodgers
Orlando, FL, USA

Writing poetry is my gift to myself and others. It keeps me centered and at peace. Each poem an author writes is an invitation to experience their thoughts and feelings. I hope you enjoy your journey with me.

Masterpiece

To all committed relationships

I watched your tears fall
Like tiny crystals
Pierced by God's pure light
Revealing the kaleidoscope of colors
In your life
Your face etched finely
With the lines of time
Mapping the travel of a life so full
Boundary lines of following rules
Depth, passion, and wisdom
Have held me in your glance
Your embraces kept me in a trance
Oh, to let you know
I will follow where you go
To watch your watercolors fade
A pool of rainbow haze
My life has been spent
To witness each event
A work in progress now complete
Behold our masterpiece

J. Joy Rodgers

Artist's Profile
Jacklyn Hoard
Salamanca, NY, USA

I write poetry to reflect incidents that happen around me or to me. My poems tell a story and ultimately show my inner feelings and strengths. Many people have been touched by what I write because they too have been in similar situations, and relate to the words they read and the feelings that they convey.

Eyes of Sapphire Blue
For me

What makes you so elusive?
I wondered as I sat
Upon the wooden bench amid this shaded elm
A girl with eyes of sapphire blue and skin with pinkish glow
This woman so adorned beneath her straw-gold ribboned hat
'Tis oftentimes I see her walking quietly along
With no one by her side; it makes me sad
My wish is to approach this lady in her solitude
To put within her heart a joyful song
But something tells me do not go, be still, it is not time
Be strong, for one day, she will need that too
The day will come when you will share your life in perfect rhyme
With this woman with the eyes of sapphire blue

Jacklyn Hoard

The Task Is Done

Alone she stood, amidst the wood
With boughs and branches spreading round,
A mango tree so large and good
That sheltered men and birds around.

She bore the brunt of every strain:
The gusty wind, the freezing cold,
The scorching sun, the pouring rain,
And lightning marred her trunk of old.

Did she withhold her fruit so sweet
From traveller's thirst in torrid time,
Or denied the bees her nectar sweet?
Comes "no" from sky, her friend all-time.

But lo! One day, in greed he spied,
In bits unkind, the cutter cut down
With blood around, aloud she cried,
"The task is done" and flat fell down.

Endowed, enriched, and greatly blessed
With gifts and talents, one can ask
What gift to the giver you leave as your best
But a fruitful life of fulfilled task?

John V. G. Moodey

The Weightless

The clouds are still with my vengeance.
In years past they droned in silence,
Humming their wispy memories to
Deafened ears.
But Man gave no moments of time
And greedily sought the open light,
Unveiled and wild in its fury.
And seeing this, the stratus wept.
But tears with mere gravity break,
Steam on the boiling arms of men
Outstretched to the star, striving
For eternity. . . .
When darkness fell upon my fellowman,
I cursed the clouds with fury,
For their apathy, their dissonance,
Their weightless raining tears.

Ignacio Bayardo Peña

The Wild Dogs

Near dusk the path still shimmered
when made flaccid by the sun. We
craved the silent blue of St. Paul's
Bay. Orange earth drier than powder
sifted over our sandals. The old
screams of cicadas filled us, then
came the slow howling. It was there
long before us, the rib cage, the snarls.
The wild dogs stalked us. We swam,
three dots below the cliff. One dog
eyeing us snapped after fish in the
shallows. The sun fell fast, the water
darkened, seemed to deepen. The pillars
of the temple struck up into the sky;
white marble cut that sunset like
teeth.

Lisa Sopka

A Time for Sleep

To my mother Lynda, for her strength and love

A half-made sandwich sits on the kitchen counter
where hunger and exhaustion from an eternal night
finally beat her into leaving her post in the rocking chair;
the doctor's final commission on a life soon to end,
where another regret begins.
Upstairs, two small boys sleep soundly, dreaming of flight
over grassy fields and a land of dinosaurs,
unaware that the house has just dimmed.

He holds his tiny son
in a large wooden rocking chair that never fails.
The working hands that built a life in this blue house are
helpless, incapable of repair. They gently hold this little
bundle and fail to keep it warm for the first time.
She approaches slowly with tear-stained cheeks and tired eyes.
He carefully puts three years back in her arms one more time.
She carries him upstairs for her final task and tucks him in,
knowing the blankets and sheets will stay in the crib this time.

The boys rub sleep from their tired eyes
wondering why they are up so early, and why her eyes are red.
She tells them to say goodbye to their playmate,
the second letter in their morning ABCs.
Then back to sleep, not to wake for fifteen years.

Justin Hirota

Artist's Profile
Malcolm Mejin
Kuching, Malaysia

This poem is like a warm cup of chicken broth, soothing the body within. Comparing nature with human life, this poem affirms that no matter how gloomy or depressed a soul can be, there is always comfort and light in the end because life is full of its mystical mysteries. I hope that this poem offers encouragement to others overcoming plights and trials, as it has enlightened and rekindled my spirit.

A New Horizon
To Mom and Dad

As the dark sky fades into bright brilliance,
My mind travels on a magical path,
Penetrating into another world behind the horizon.
The sun of new life has just begun.
My feet are soaring like wings,
My soul gains way to newness and anticipation.

The heinous struggles have left me.
All the icy pasts spare my sanity.
The roaring seas of danger I have overcome,
The sadistic strains of reality have blossomed into strength.
The sky was once in its darkest gloom,
The sun was seemingly hidden for eternal doom.
The picture of the sky was an abominable sight,
Everything seems to have lost its glory of life.

But dusk arrives like in a shining armor of light and hope.
The majestic sun glows and rises like a phoenix from ashes.
The sunrays give strength and newness,
Darkness has no chains and controls.
It is time to leave the dusts of time behind and move on.
A new life has just begun again,
Just beyond that beautiful horizon.

Malcolm Mejin

Crabapple Tree

I am the return of fruit
absorbed my fine mesh of root
as stem, seed, meat.
I am the budding again from
old scars, freeing life from

wounds and hardening my flesh
in layers against cold years. These rings
I have pushed beyond my center,
like a bell finally entering the minds
of my disciples, who sink into meditation,

and escape from internal voice-overs.
I am the whirling with fruit . . .
like red sequins, or tiny maracas. . . .
I am the radiating and the rippling
forth, a ripe sun for anyone's taking.

Adam Lavitt

Red-Tongued Clay

To and unyielding love of life

I want your red-tongued clay
painted on cow lily fields of gold,
my hair flying free over vast
plots of undying fern.
You let me exist
in my own existence
without the weight of you,
pre-existing love affairs.
My daffodil-touched mountains
and foam-drenched seas,
bleached desert sand.
We cross the barren into the whetted
meadows of sparkling pink,
and your red-tongued clay
passing oceans of depth.

Kathryn McRee

single parent
my divorce

in the dark crimson glow
of the chili christmas lights
on the rubber plant
lies are told in silence
to a slow bossa nova
on the other side of her eyes
an upside-down mirror image
of sweetness
a dry wind across a cold empty
space in the west
a shadowing lying across
what never happened
over and over

goodbye
may you be happy

Khepran M. Mathes

In Your Eyes I Want to Cry

To Kristin Hunter

The taste of time
Innocent stream
Aspiring to be free

Or a lone peasant
Who's harvesting
The love of life foreseen

A passionate doorway
In one's own diary
By purer every day
Yet still amorous softly

Not a laugh
But not a cry
Our dreamy lullaby
Into our hearts
Where we bequeath
Our love they will abide

And through any sorrow
Or any vows forlorn
Unyielding lovers fortify
Thus forever is born

Ryan Rhode

Shattered Stalemate

I'm not inspired by your words of woe
nor the toxic tears of your ashen eyes
pouring pity upon a silken face
lived without remorse upon mankind

Your chaos is your own, not mine,
seething through your every pore
shadowed only by the arrogance
that you are the master of us all

Splinters of your sadistic deeds
sent upon my aura shall not take,
for the mirror returned it unto thee
my will is my own, not yours to take

I shall be golden among the indigo,
soaring above it all, alive and free
while you fall from the throne of bones,
left beneath your religion's withering tree

Tamara N. Fox

Untitled
To David L.

When your blessing touched my skin,
cool water, the only thing between that touch,
I felt you brush my soul
and truly bless it.

Though your god and church aren't mine,
I felt your prayer,
unarticulated and unexpressed,
like a shock of the cold water
that brushed from your fingertips
against my forehead.

The strength of your faith
has revived mine,
though I cannot convey it.

The thought and the touch of that prayer
linger against the nerves of my soul,
soft, sweet, and strong,
more intimate than if you'd kissed me.

Allison Silver

Arab Woman

To my mother and Aunt Aisha

In a small house in Tripoli lives
an ocean of wisdom. Watching her
motions, years of repetition have
perfected her skills. Her little
secrets make this daunting task
almost easy. Having raised her
babies, spent some sixty-odd years
sensing the world, sharing smiles,
advice, recipes . . . having discovered
the secrets of what makes the
world's axis spin, she knows that a
simple touch can bring comfort to a
restless mind; a smile bring ease
to a searching soul, with words,
make hearts strong. She does not
live life retrospectively; every day
a different chance to manifest into
a butterfly. Roaming the Earth has
left her delicate feet chapped, but
when dawn breaks, she smiles, stands,
and readies herself for the new day.
I stare in awe, watching her pray,
and pray that one day, I too will
have the wisdom of the Arab woman.

Howaida M. Werfelli

Untitled

I want to run from these green-gray office walls
into the drizzly wet dusk
and dance through the traffic
to the swish and thump of wiper blades,

tear off my clothes and gyrate
to the primal drumbeat
of water being slapped from glass
in technological precision,

my body flickering
in the hazy glow of headlights
as I twirl from car to car
in a prayer dance

until, at last, I collapse,
curled up, shivering on the asphalt,
smiling up at the clouds,
thankful for rain

Thomas J. P. O'Brien

Waiting

Staring at midnight walls
understanding nothing
and the time is standing tall.

Feeling understood by nobody,
it's all too often expressed
when I'm feeling low and empty
and my head has come undressed.

Standing in a statue stance
with a hint of mirror lights,
I will stand in this paradise
until the morning dance.

Scrolling to the music,
this time I know my way,
but I still have to wait
until another day.

Kevin Taylor

Unanswerable
To Dad

I think of you at absurd times,
while steaming broccoli, for instance.
"Drink all the juice," you'd say,
"That's where the vitamins are."
I roll my eyes and think,
man, take a multivitamin.
As years roll by,
your advice is more valued;
however, you make less sense
and are more difficult to convince.
Stubbornly you show your ways,
as you sit and smoke countless times,
and drink the cheap wine in six-packs.
I place the flowers on a pole,
working gingerly to place straight,
I search for a particular grace.
I understood that you were trying
to erase life.
Now helpless, I stumble each day
to say goodbye.

Janice Chilton

Artist's Profile
Makenze Holley
Bellevue, NE, USA

I am twenty years old, and writing has been a passion of mine ever since I can remember. This poem is about a man I dated a very long time ago. The poem refers to how I imagine him and feel him sometimes, but he is never there. Then I remember how painful it is to imagine him and how painful it was to be with him.

Sometimes
To Mike Mitchell

Sometimes I will be standing there and
your face will flash before my eyes,
a face that I want to erase
until it is diminished into the size of a small keyhole
like the one that is on the lock to my heart.

Sometimes I will be standing there and
the smell of your body and your breath
will float beneath my nose,
until I am lost in a memory of our lips becoming one,
like a caterpillar emerging into a butterfly.

Sometimes I will be standing there and
you will be standing in a mirage beside me,
a cloud of longing, a want to touch,
until I remember what it means to touch you;
it's like a hand placed upon a scalding fire.

Sometimes I will be standing there and
I'll be wishing that the thoughts of you
would become absent from my mind,
until I remember that I don't know how to let you go,
like a sinner, begging for their unfaithful life.

Makenze Holley

Zoe

She floats on a canvas, soft and fair
Her life a torrent of love rushing
Coursing over colored stones
Merging with the swelling tide

See her there astride the waves
The water moving to her dance
She clasps the mane of nature's pride
And rides the wind

And then as colors start to fade
Gathered in a cloud of white
Silken pillow for her head
She floats into the night

Seth George Anawalt

Truro Dune Harmony

Black jays with orange-hinged wings
skeet across a dune marsh
as dusk deepens to begin.

Sky arcs one million azure miles
above this curve of coastline,
dune cliffs block the sunset,
which hues the northern sky in tiers.

The horizon-wall, tone after tone,
peaks and drains in bars of color,
a tuning of radiance for hours
from a treasure horde older than humans.

A brown and white spotted gull
poised beneath a pink dune cliff
waits for its moment to nest.

Gregg Mosson

Failing

For Therese

The flesh has been a decade failing, months to years
of daily loss.

She watches dying with her eyes
flashing fire, sparking hope,
but speaks of ending in
a voice warmed with whispers.

At midnight my phone rings
to chant the litany . . .
children, lovers, doctors,
no miracles among them.
Then she asks the only question:
how much have you loved me?

Enough, I say.
Now, too much.

Jody Serey

Quay
To N.

We're sitting on the quay
trying to out spit each other, Ron and me.

The waves are lulling the hits
up and down, up and down,
no bullseye, or misses.

The sun is aloof today, in a mist,
just light and warm, but no sweat.
No glare or burn as last month,
just a slight breeze between our shoulders.

Our tongues feel heavy
in the late afternoon.
Summer makes for lazy minds

and limp limbs . . . and spitting
only makes our mouths drier.

Iliya Patev

Moonstone

Silver plays of light hypnotizing . . .
Tiny figures stream in through the trees.
Every leaf, every shake casts a new silhouette,
And the dancers soon hypnotize me.

Can't sleep but for this sense of longing,
Can't dream or my spirit runs dry.
Heart bound to body, body bound to earth,
Soul longing to conquer the sky.

Dancers spin round on my pillow,
Beckoning me please to come soon.
Trying to locate the source of their might . . .
In the heavens above me, the moon.

No longer does sunlight escape me,
Nor does sleep elude my grasp.
My moonlight, sweet savior, embrace me,
Leave loneliness caught in the past.

Julia Eileen Lindley

A Woman Left Unkissed

A woman, unkissed, curls up around her edges,
Like an old photograph left in the rain and dried by the sun.
Colors fading, she slips into the ashes
Where her love once burned.

Anna Elizabeth Clay

Tree of Lamentation

She's not the tallest of trees,
And has an awkward countenance
Bending slightly to the left.
Yet elves don't reject her.
They dally unseen at her feet
Where she digs her limbs into the earth.
Her upper branches provide a resting place
For melancholy fairies to sing their lament.
If she were human, her slip would be showing.
From her oversized purse would come butterscotch drops,
A handkerchief and odd scribble notes.
In summer, her branches grow hard talons.
In winter, she is brilliant, white, and soft.
And ancient being is this tree
Who is called "Pinus Nigra"
But I shall call her Grace,
For she is sentinel to unseen magic,
And companion to those who
Rest unsteady on terra firma.

Patricia Ann Rule

The Girl by the Sea
To my sister

There is a girl by the seashore sitting
And raising her head with a winsome look.
For a moment she forgets her knitting.

Resembling a maid from a storybook,
She leans on the back of her wicker chair
And lays aside her little knitting hook.

The gentle sea breeze blows her raven hair
As spraying mists bedew her big blue eyes.
A smile on her face makes her look so fair,

That knowing look that somehow mystifies.

Jacqueline Terrence Shartrand

The Cat Speaks

Your hungry eyes are searching for
a word, a glimpse, a hint
of what you believe exists in me,
what you've wagered your sanity on.
Sometimes I think I see it
and shyly offer you the shadow I've found.
Sometimes you rejoice in the chance that your wager is won,
sometimes you recoil in anger. . . .
The shadow was just a shadow.
So your eyes grow ever hungrier
as you wait with sweet words for me to appear
and shyly offer another shadow,
a word, a glimpse, a hint
of the stranger I might be.

Karilyn Warsinski

Sentinel

To my husband

She inhales,
Great sighs blowing the papers from my desk.
Then she is still, absorbing the oxygen into
The hollows deep underground and high overhead.

You can almost imagine a pulse,
As if ruby liquid rushed through thick plaster skin,
Nutrients supplying brain and brawn
That she may stand another century.

Protector of her domain,
Her bones creak as they're walked upon.
Careful as you stride to climb her ligaments
That none are loose or broken.

Her large eyes lay wide open
Even in the depths of slumber.
The big bulking beast sprawls out,
Stretching her hulking body over 3000 square feet.

She lies still like a great dragon on the knoll,
Watching defensively as I arrive home.

H. Sony Hutson-Tawney

Artist's Profile
Lena L. Bowling
Bethel, OH, USA

I am twenty-three years old. I wrote this poem after I was divorced in February of this year. I had always blamed and just been so angry at my ex-husband for everything that I never took the time to enjoy the good things we had in our time together. Now I have come to see that happiness isn't always waiting for me to find it; sometimes it is in the moments you forget to enjoy. I wrote this with that in mind, because my ex is still my friend and we do have good memories, as friends should.

The Pursuit of Happiness

Chasing rainbows and gold
Running always to the better tomorrow
I missed out on my wonderful todays
Seeking enlightenment on a false path
Hoping for brighter days
Forgoing the ones I turned into yesterdays
Looking out into the great beyond
Dreaming of so much to explore
I took for granted all that I already discovered
Reaching for the warmth of memories now
Clinging to happier times
Surely forgetting creating those memories
Now wondering why
So caught up in searching for happiness
I lost sight of it in front of me
There among the "wasted time"
Laid out before me
Yet I was too blind to see
My pursuit was in vain
Happiness was always there
Chasing me

Lena L. Bowling

shattered glass

balloons have never swelled to this size before,
the size where hearts are broken,
millions of pieces splintered.
the hands swelling from pain.

each ring from afar,
a darting spoil
shot through walls and indefinable circumstances,
each bringing water to the eyes.

it's unimaginable,
a shower of words can't be said.
the nuisance of the outside world betrays me
and slices of hope
are taken piece by piece,
eaten away by passion.

Julia Au

Truce

We were two children
sitting in a warm moon shadow,
breathing truceful air
of pine needles.
We were two dots
revolving in cold space
as planets came and went with
a rumble.
We were two giants
sitting on kingdoms,
listening to the footfalls
of a thousand tiny feet.
We were nonexistent,
watching mechanical lighted birds
carry precious cargo
to their destinations.
We were silent,
saying more than a million words,
sitting in a warm moon shadow.

Nancy Buck

Cosmic Pallet

To Larry Albright and Lincoln Glen Church, a place of inspiration

He takes His brush,
Mixes His never-ending pallet,
Pours it upon the Earth.
Mixing, swirling, ever-changing,
A kaleidoscope made only for me.
A wonder, a blessing on mortal sight,
He creates the night
While all colors fade to gray.
All vibrancy simply an illusion,
A remembrance of times past,
He pierces the cloud of darkness
With His celestial pinprick.
Darkness calls, brings one and all,
The death of light, the draw of night,
Brings crippling fright as an awesome sight.
The night is mended as the dawn breaks.
The great tailor repairs the pinpricks of luminescence,
He folds the black cover of night and stores it for another time.
The painter begins anew.
The beauty of day, the mystique of night,
All pale to the transition.
Sunrise, sunset.

Bryan Ringsted

Autumn's Grace

Autumn's intrepid grace
Flows auspiciously
To fulfill its embrace.

The last gasps of color shout
Over the landscape,
While chilled whispers play out.

The cackling flock
Carves through Heaven's mist,
Following a precedent clock.

Dried remnants of a stream
Thirst for moisture.
Nature's relief will be extreme.

All stands right with the world.
Soon winter's icy fingers
Will incase our lives, as a pearl.

Darell Hine

Hollins Hill
To quiet travelers

Solid brick houses
bloom on grassy mounds,
only two;
must have been a cool summer.

A small patch of farms
drinks late morning
through splintered roots.

The silos grew tall this year.

Fat ponies waft by,
planting hooves and manes
while trees and shrubs
stand about, betting
on which crop will become
the sturdiest mare.

As I observe from Hollins Hill,
my sitting bones embed
deep into moist soil.
I blossom, imbibing
these swaying moments
in soft wind and seedy sunlight.

Jessica Suzanne McGlew

Blue Light Special

Buzzing through the poorly-lit aisles,
People contemplating their shopping lists.
The stampeding of eager feet
Resonating through the high ceiling,
Sounding like thunder.
Garrulous eager bodies looking for the perfect buy.
One bustling buyer browses through bathroom towels,
Running her worn hands over the soft cotton.
Through her thick red glasses she watches
An old Michael Jackson album fall to the ground.
A pneumatic leg nonchalantly crushes it with her pointed heels.
An employee in a dark blue smock
Quickly sweeps it up, cautiously,
Not to be stampeded by the eager shoppers.
"Today's blue light special is on aisle 9,"
Shouts a morose voice over the loudspeaker.
A cattle-like herd of bargain searchers sprints down the aisle
To pluck the last of the bargain waffle irons
Off the shelves of K-Mart.

Janelle Crandall

Artist's Profile
Richard Lewis Beal
London, United Kingdom

This poem is like a mental picture of the days that I spent in Toba City on the east coast of Japan in December 2002. A few months prior, I had started playing the saxophone, and really wanted to play by the sea. There are also accompanying photos that were taken at the time. This poem endeavors to capture the thoughts, atmosphere, and feelings that I had at that time. I hope that other people will similarly be able to visualize this or relate it to their own experiences of being by the sea.

Sax on the Beach
To the sea

I stood out on that empty shore
To contemplate the world at sea.
With sax in hand I saw for miles
And felt as free as one can be.

Waves rolled and met with sandy beach
Whilst I depressed its yellow keys.
Out came soft tunes with fuzzy sounds,
A mixture of breath and sea breeze.

And so the tide washed over sand,
All alone save for some trees,
Thus my solo was its only muse,
Yet music flowed with flawless ease.

Just by myself I stared away
At yonder world where ships have gone,
And playing heartfelt tunes I made,
I realized how our worlds were one.

Richard Lewis Beal

the ragman

the rags on the pavement,
be it for a moment, then gone
as the wind sweeps across the crowded stone tiles,
swooped by an invisible hand
casting them skyward to scatter
wherever fate drops its darts.
on the hilltop overlooking the urban
rooftops
stands the ragman; on each rag is written
secret somethings before he one by one
lets the wind
wherever these rags may randomly fall,
the blessed few are like magnets, while
others chase to collect.

Mads Nielsen

Eye of the Storm

It's quiet,
devastating.
She's surrounded by hundreds of people
but standing alone.
A car alarm goes off in the distance,
only she knows.
It's deafening.
There's a small boy
screaming for his mother.
His lips move without sound
as he circles the area,
feeling for an invisible hand.
A glass falls behind her.
It shatters and broken glass spills across the floor,
small crystals fall below her feet.
A barely noticeable twinge of disappointment
crosses the owner's face.
She turns quickly as a stranger
knocks her with his shoulder.
She hears the high-pitched ring of the car alarm,
the cry of the child as his mother
races to hold his hand,
the scraping of the glass being swept off the floor.

Mika Haberlin

In Remembrance

For Amy Lee and Dean, now more than ever

I had you like a photograph, grey . . .
Or perhaps an old old portrait, fading into the
Vague. An insecure recollection.
Did your mouth curl into a shriveled smile
Or did you stare, unblinking, at the flash of my brain,
Gluing the amber moment into my cerebral photo frame?

I stand outside on the grass and gather together
The mossy memory of you, and with a sting
It pinches me that you are on the other side of the house
Hung above a fireplace, and kept in a shoe box;
Your socks, a rotted rose petal, bloodshot from weeping
And a drawing, reminding me.

This is all I can say in words.

Jennifer L. McFarland

Ashes

I gingerly stammer towards your ghost
Remember the taste of your hateful glaze
As daunting is this stagnant garden
The phantoms float away in haste

Did I plan to sustain this
A trifle hammer in my midst
I swerve to miss vehement risk
And all that's left is sacrifice

I chase the shroud and it takes its toll
Swaying in the rhetoric
I take my cue and trace my steps
Am I still tethered to your ghost

I gingerly stagger towards your ghost
And revel in past argument
You wonder what's behind the Band-Aid
The only answer is regret

Lisa Lewis

Artist's Profile
Andrew Parrish
Las Cruces, NM, USA

This piece represents the action of motion in the mind of dancers as they prepare to present. As a dancer myself, I truly appreciate the feelings of anticipation and the full relief of completion. The full release is only found in a faithful audience that watches me carefully and appreciates what I have to say through my body.

The Dance

To the spirit of dance

I'm standing here in a crowded wing,
But still feeling alone in my nervousness.
I am in a moment of silence,
A moment of butterflies.
The lights dim, the audience quiets.
Stage lights up! Music go!
The butterflies, once felt before,
Are now rushing in earnest.
Carefully, I extend my foot,
Pushing my ankle through.
Is the audience aware? What are they expecting?
Too soon, I find myself finished,
And backstage once again.
The butterflies have left . . .
Replaced by a rush of satisfaction,
Loving the moment of release in movement,
Cherishing the memory.

Andrew Parrish

Dreamed Snares

Enthrall me with imagined kisses
And sweet dreamed caresses
You have usurped my senses
And ravished my unwary heart
It beats for you now
Overthrown are my defenses
Erected in your absence
Unknowingly turned into my trap
Ensnared with fantasies
Of your calm embrace
And gentle enticing thoughts
Break my spirit
Or trap me anew
And yet you cannot see me
Caught in my dreams of you

Siobhán Greaney

Looked Out

Closing in and it's all around me.
I can feel it all moving beyond earth and willow boughs.
Tied to this is the design of origin.

How you make moonbeams
turn into sand
on a winter beach.

I miss the ideas that used to extend far
out to the flares and bursts in the
sun's good mornings.

Having caught those rays,
those sueded hips of
chewy cabernet,
my eyes are left juxtaposing,
predicated nouns and
past participles.

Robbin Lynn Alfred

The Flute

Whispered endearments
are delivered at my ear
that flow in my whole being,
though impossible to hear.
Vibrations expand within me,
searching for their likes outside,
creating a harmonious concert
when emerging to the other side.
Thus I become a cherished instrument,
a perfectly designed little flute.
Your breath travels through me,
making music while I remain mute.

Rocio Aguilar Anzures

Echoes of Me

She is echoes of me,
and I envy her,
safe and laughing,
curious and happy,
content and adventurous,
an explorer of dreams
within reality.
Now I am an explorer
of reality through dreams.
That is my safety
but not my laughter.
That she keeps for herself,
holding it fast
while I numbly wrestle
with myself and with her
for just a piece
of what she holds,
for without it I fear
I am an echo of her,
for she is bright and whole
where I bleed into pieces
too bright to be seen.

Joanna Lucy Curtis

Services Rendered

Searching through coat pockets
For a pen to fill out forms
To obtain his release
From a weeklong hospital stay
Instead found a rumpled package of stale cigarettes.

A sudden cardiac occurrence
Reached inside his chest and refused to let go
Until he lay pale and lifeless
Next to the checkout desk.

Afterward, a person with impeccable manners
Approached and asked discreetly,
As one might during a situation such as this,
About the large bill incurred by his bout with pneumonia
The week before.

Politely responding with a firmness and demeanor.
Directly in contrast with my accustomed style.

He would very much wish to disburse payment
For services rendered, but unfortunately,
His government pension is now terminated
Due to the death of the recipient.

Edward Jones

A Wooden Temptress

Before today, he always sat with a wicker violin,
The loose string wrapped around his fingers.
It had not been used in decades, but was still worth gold.
His fingers, dangling and motionless, were hung by the chords.
Chords of Eden, they say he was once a god among men.
The sweet, angelic voices pray to be fixed, tightened,
But the numb hand only lies, deceives them again.
He says their voices will sing once again,
But only lies remain true.
It never happens, it never did, for decades.
Someone had to fix it, to right the wrong.
I took action, I made a mistake.
I tightened the strings, and off came his fingers.

Brandon Brown

Artist's Profile
Aisha N. Alford
Bridgeport, CT, USA

Well, I wouldn't call myself a poet, but I do like to write poems as I feel them come on. My inspirations can come from anywhere, like making a bet that I couldn't write a poem about something or my daughter being just herself. This is just a good example of what I love to do.

Tears

I've held them so long
they burst now
through amber strokes,
greens, saturated reds, and
shades of blue
reminding me of the water I run to.
Exploding hot and lavalike,
running,
clinging to the slope of my cheek,
carrying my pain and my joy.
The more I attempt to wipe them away
the more they come,
flooding my lips, clouding
my thoughts,
leaving behind a valley of salt
empty and devoid of moisture.
Life then replenishes them
and the process starts all over again.

Aisha N. Alford

Green Glass
To my all

In a scare,
Brown lights in my eyes,
I stood before shimmering green glass. . . .
In a stare,
I couldn't distinguish where the skies
Separated endlessly from green grass.
Clouds felt heavy,
They'd push my ribs back on me every time I'd breathe in.
I reached out to relieve them.
The weatherman misinformed me of a downpour to begin.
Sweet sour pearls
Rolled off to edges dressed in dull blonde lashes,
Dampening its curls,
The core of my soul burnt, dust into ashes.
My fingers traced down teardrops,
Streams carving down through the hills of your cheek
And long before it stopped,
Mountains in the background were tumbling from the peak.
As the portrait suicided
I was faster to the floor,
Saved the parts undivided,
And again I saw the rain;
Only time had partly dried it.

Doha Mohammad Matar

fearing salmonella

drove home that night
with the stereo off
a tremor herald for
violent voice quakes
rending silent earth

tried to boil myself
in the shower while
gnawing through knees
but then got out
toweled off
and planned to
buy you flowers

wrapped my mind in
red red red
roses all night
under an eggshell moon
lidless eyes
cracked the dawn
spilling a yolk sun

i kept the secret:
they only had orange ones

Hunter O'Brien

Today
To Adrian

After reading "Anna Karenina"
I picture her face
under the train
the peasant muttering as she jumped
and was pulled downward

And today in a Houston high rise
I realize I ruined myself
not for passion
but for money
and all is lost

I walk to Main Avenue
pass Foley's empty-headed mannequins
and watch the metro train
tracks slick from rain
and think of you

Juanita Mantz

Heartbreaking Nature

Where the sharp land drops its white coat
Starts to run a sterile stream.
Its potential is to float
Never scratched by dirt or gleam.
Yet the surface's scarce of smoothness,
Cliffs for shaving, stones to shear;
Every one of them is waiting
In a pile, the stream to spear.
How dare the water flush them
To their bones in quickened epochs.
Its mega tonic currents cleave
The diamond sharpness of the rocks.
So degrading of the solids
To arrange the densest legion.
Fearless boulders shield and veil
The guerrilla pebbles' region.
Equal shame to the liquid:
Droplets always on the run.
They are soldiers armed with Newtons,
Undulation from each gun.
During impact, water taints,
Every brave rock loses sand.
Oh, how peaceful is the sound
Of a gentle stream on land.

Michael Solovyov

Blades

The plastic fan in my window
hums louder than the crickets . . .
but girls love their creature comforts.
The fan in our kitchen
had three lights . . .
one never worked
and it made a rusty clank,
so after ten years we replaced it
and now the room's too bright.
My brother and I dared each other,
then double dared,
to touch the blades on Grandma B's whirring blue fan
and we laughed 'til I broke my pinkie.
Once, when I thought no one was watching,
I stood in front of the fan in the bathroom
and let my (then) blonde hair fly as I made my movie star face
and wished for bigger lips.
Now a lazy ceiling fan overhead
casts yawning shadows over my bed
in its rhythmic pattern which I've adopted as my own,
tapping my foot to the mechanical sound
until I switch it off at night
and sweat.

Katie Bernot

one last moment
to the vibes of life

just to think about a tale of reality,
then to discover a glimpse of humanity
waiting relentlessly for the river streams to meet,
i waited all spring with bare empty hands

i never knew till i discovered by chance,
to love someone is not a will of heart
people meet and shadows fade away,
it is only when the birds sing i cry your name

so cruel is the mind of reality
when it uncovers its face of immortality
to stand aside the picture of two frames,
the depths so maternal, the colors so same

the delicate drops of rain as they touch the craving ground,
their desire to be absorbed, or a need of time
shining are the streets at night, acting as an infamous mirror
the reflections that i see through them
await for one last moment

Syed Muslim Abbas

Artist's Profile
David Farley
San Francisco, CA, USA

I am a thirty-two-year-old poet and aspiring author, currently writing my second novel and driving a taxicab in beautiful San Francisco, California. I've published several poetic works in various anthologies by the International Library of Poetry, and look to soon publish the longer narratives, both of which are poetry driven. My untitled poem in this edition is representative of a form of "catalytic evocation" meant to germinate as a possibility of change in the mind of the reader . . . portraying enigmas of consciousness and reveling in universal questions each reader answers for themselves.

untitled

deep in the unconscious collective
our body speaks through nerve webs
in the dialect of astral origins
beyond intellects
cool quarrel reason
we lose ourselves
to getting lost in ourselves
while our place in the universe
is always perfect
and our fantasies
our lustrous metaphors
carry us across
the fences of what we fear
to believe
to hope
to dare
our slumber dreams
our subconscious maps
vaguely mystify
but rarely realize
more than our waking world
but our waking dreams
exempt from what seems
are the fables of what if

David Farley

Santa Barbara

The mountains bump against the morning,
Reminding me that they are there.
At noon the sun melts into poppies
Riding the hills sliding to the sea.
By four, the breeze for homing sailors
Has caught the salt of the coming tide
And flavors the city air with the taste of ocean.
The setting sun's fire licks the islands
As they lie dark upon the water like diehard surfers
Awaiting that one final wave before nightfall.
In the quiet of evening, Orion, the Pleiades,
Taurus, or Cassiopeia blink against the night sky
While the moon rides at rest.
And I and my dreams, like flotsam, softly float
Upon a whispering quiet
Until the early tide debarks from shore
As dawn draws away from night,
Leaving the day as bared as the night wet sand.

Kathleen Roxby

Broken Glass

Blind velvet surrounds my liquid heart
The rhythm of your lips has me begging for more
I blush listening to your glass secrets
An angel haunting me for eternity
In a pool of champagne you linger on and let me drag
But this time I cannot devour the change
My concrete heart was broken by your morning smile

Olga Rozman

frost-forming hours

the frost-forming hours of the night
during which i usually drive home
an apple in an orchard of bones
only i know the heart is there
tones descending in the distance
on the highway
maybe if we keep all the vehicles moving
the ice streaks on the windows
won't catch us
provisional, terror and pleasure
elements in some endless larger composition
that hole still swallows, beats, practices
or is otherwise active
and like any organization of cells
exercises desire as its purpose
so i must call it something
a hollow organ

Aaron London

Hadrian

I saw the height of Hadrian's wall
That stood in front of me and at your front,
Tempted by the Siren and witching call,
Abandoning when I claimed I wouldn't.
Remember by Roman street where we played,
Running around on the emerald grass.
Not one moment was a sweet kiss displayed,
Emotions never on mind did trespass.
The antique air filled with the smell
Of the rain clouds with the mid-summer wind.
My heart did collapse when we said farewell,
Lips no longer touched, grin no longer grinned.

Leaving, I looked at you and you at me
And never will our two eyes be one see.

Steven L. Decker

untitled

the question, not will i be an extremist,
but
what will i be an extremist for?
champion of a cause of justice?
an extremist for love?
leader or follower?
silent majority or hated and
misunderstood
vocal minority?
champion of the poor?
healer of the sick?
brightener of the unsmiling?
lover of the unwanted
and unloved?
talker or doer?
a line must
be

drawn

John Marion

Day after Day

You may want to run away at times, but know you can't run from life

I come to this place
where the trees are alive and green
to visit the wooden bench hidden beneath the shade
as the sound of children laughing lingers in the air
clashing with the rumble of the city streets

I dreamt of this place
when I was young and hurting for freedom
To get lost in its diversity and individuality of
skyscrapers, street entertainers, and taxis
running from the captivity of the memories polluting my mind

I see children playing games in Sheep's Meadow
How wonderful it would be to be that naive and innocent again
to remember when life was that simple and
happiness was not a fairy tale

I pray with closed eyes and a broken heart
I feel a breeze tickle my spine and as I take in a breath
of fresh air, my burdens disappear into the summer wind

Vanessa Walden

Artist's Profile
Bobbi Danielle Goldner
Las Vegas, NV, USA

When I was writing this poem, it was a response to a challenge. It tells of the world in a highly oversensitive perception of colors and senses. It's meant to show the different sides and personalities of people and how well they can fit inside the conformed world.

Multicolored Soul

I want to be wrapped
in your satin blue
comforted by your wooly skin
that itches mine
yet warms my inner being
Your green eyes pierce my skin
burning my flesh off the bones
dancing the horrific tango of fire
Yellow fields of daisies in my mind
a garden of warm memories satisfied
with the clouds' sweet tears
Chocolate fudge melts in my mouth
dripping from my ruby lips
daring you to touch and taste
the colors I bleed and feel
An indigo rainbow punctures the sky
the colors melting into one another
a mixture of bonds into one color
Pink kisses flutter on my eyelashes
teasing my blotched face with tears
Your multicolored soul blends well
with the world's shell
that I can't tell
which is yours and which is mine

Bobbi Danielle Goldner

Artist's Profile
Karishma Sinha
Plano, TX, USA

This poem was written for the very first time when I was a sixteen-year-old. Even though this version is rewritten and edited rather mercilessly by me now, I have tried to preserve its essence. Thank you so much for all your encouragement and faith in these humble inspirations of mine, for that is all they are.

Starving Blossom

To children who live and die on the streets, starved and ignored

Stare out the car window through
A tinted glass. It protects me from
The flower child outside.
Her grubby face pressed against
The shield
Displaying her merchandise:
A blood red rose from
Early spring.
Tiny feet scalded and torn . . . toes up
To peer inside.
She begs me with contempt and
Large beautiful eyes.
I finger the coins in my leather purse,
Mesmerized.
Two seconds till I can hand her the
Money, the light turns green.
I utter a cry of protest but the
Chauffeur ignores me.
Speeding away to a marble fort I
Console my guilty soul.
Next time maybe the light won't turn
Green before my greedy hands
Can perform that forgotten act
Called charity.

Karishma Sinha

on my way home

the tracks of oases shallowly passed crossed
single tracks meandering everywhere in all
directions windblown undoing of the ties our
feet bind no don't go stop there will be no
track no footprint revisited in the vast and
empty wilderness please make your mark tie
your knot the fixedness we attach to stars
is just our way of making our way home

Dave Parrella

Boy on a Swing

The plastic seat buckles,
attached to the chains.
He sits; it is just another day.
Clothes are tattered, hair a knotted mess,
hasn't had a shower for at least a month.
Face stares, stern, any
light in his eyes was dampened,
extinguished long ago.
Ripped shoes push from the wood chips,
flying, faint movement of his lips appears.
Light shining from his eyes,
just reflection from the sun.
He is free, if only for a little while,
still held to the earth by a chain.
Voices soon shatter his dream,
families appear, their accusing eyes
burning inside him.
The ride is over, he has to leave,
returning to the world he has come from,
the one on the street.

Natasha Laird

Dream

I see a world
with lavender skies
and clouds made from the white birch
tree in my yard.
They drip silver earrings
that melt upon contact
with the cool, green moss
that covers all land
from one coast to any other.
I envision swamps
and forests
and jungles and deserts and snowy
mountains. After eight o'clock,
the sci-fi movie set night slides by,
covering up the day
with its massive nothingness.
And with one fantastic breath
I take it in.
Blink.

It's gone.

Kayla Rosebrook

Below Lamplight

Light is enigmatic,
it covets solitude,
smiles when it pleases,
grows against the vermilion of leaves
and the grey-green of slow moss over boulders.
Light creeps
around my head, like a crown:
I am Caesar,
I am Jesus,
I bleed roses and spurt conquests . . .
and the light grows over me,
a lamp
with the moon
encased in the womb of its breath.
Here, I will await you.
In your voice
are the caprices of spring,
in my petals, your tragedies.
I will stand,
a queen in a king's skin,
my rights folded into my corset,
singing like a dictator.

Julia Sanches

Artist's Profile

Victoria Murch

Woking, United Kingdom

This poem means a lot to me. It is about my first love, who I adored and a small part of me still does. It shows the pain of an ended relationship and how it can affect us.

Love Lost

To my first love

The pain so deep, so breathless,
My body strains to bear,
Eyes swimming in an ocean,
The tides they can't contain.
The left quarter of my frame
Begins to throb through every nerve.
A toddler could make walking look easy,
I can only manage to shuffle.
Looking around the world slowly,
Yet seeing like a blind man,
The pain will pass, I assume;
Until then, I leave my vulnerability to the world.

Victoria Murch

Artist's Profile
Christopher D. Fisher
Decatur, IL, USA

This piece is an observation of the magnificence of creation demonstrated from God as it permeates through me, my mind, and the universe. It is an attempt to commemorate the glorious universe within each individual.

Spiral

Twirling, whirling epitome of cyclic infinity.
Concentric, eccentric, wrapping 'round with perfect symmetry.
Ah, spiral!
Embodiment of the self-revolving, always-evolving mind
That accelerates at an undefined pace
Yet simultaneously creating space
As he contorts higher and higher,
Longer, yet stronger from his seminal womb.
Spiral of the world, creator and destroyer.
From the microcosmic, ubiquitous double helix, he spans
All the way to galactic proportions he demands,
Dwarfing stars like atoms.
Spiral!
Let him spin, encircling life, elevating with every twist,
Following only the path he set before despite strife;
Who could have imagined this?
Growing, never slowing, taller so wild,
Connecting this innocent brainchild
To ever-expanding wavelengths of knowledge.
Indiscernible to limited linears who even went to college.
Spiral!
Kinky, ever so slinky celebration of the circle.

Christopher D. Fisher

Artist's Profile
Connie Voog
Aitkin, MN, USA

Being born and raised in Minnesota means being surrounded by nature and all her wonder and beauty. My mother always taught me the meaning of such beauty and its price. Our closely-knit relationship has been the sole purpose and tribute to her life. She has deeply not only myself, but many who knew her. May the Lord bless your lives as she rests in peace.

Mother Earth . . . Spring

To my mother, Lois Cable

Waking, she lifts her arms to the sun,
Pausing to shake her shoulders
And brushing sleep from her eyes.

White trillium and yellow marsh marigolds
Bloom abundant at her feet
Replacing white crystalline wrap.

Animal babies stir in her forest
Filling each room with new sounds
Under fresh leaves canopy cover.

Birds' migration fills the crisp air
Their raucous calls add a beauty song
Bounteous color on feathered wings.

Narcissus raises triumphant heads
Kissed by radiant sunlight
Anticipating the first spring rain.

Earthy humus thawing in layers
Welcoming tightly wound fronds
Releasing tension in a windy sigh.

Connie Voog

Artist's Profile
Sarah Williams
Pismo Beach, CA, USA

My grandmother is full of such unparalleled life and grace, despite her age. When she is tending to her garden, she is no longer a old woman; rather, she is ageless, beautiful. The roses and the other growing things bend to her will, as she is their keeper, the giver of their life and death.

Ageless Domain

In the blue lush light of morning
she emerges, sleep-drenched, stiff
but moving with furtive grace,
body worn and tired, like the roses
that she so lovingly grooms, tangled
with age, but spiteful, determined,
to avoid the gunmetal shears
for one more year.

She sits right down,
runs her rough hands
through the espresso brown dirt,
smiles as it drips like thick water
through her cramped fingers.
Head tilted, brow furrowed, she surveys
her feathery green domain, alive
with the buzzing richness of being.

Sarah Williams

flora

wind a gentle soft whisper
daffodils that pirouette
harmonic spheres of light

golden reflections in pink coral
a topaz sea with sapphire sky
at the speed of love

waterfalls of delicate lace
on velvet moss
crested golden wood
chiming bells of orchids
with ruby roses

Francesca Judd

Weeping of the Weeds

The dandelion cursed with sentience
stares heartbreakingly at roses towering above,
yearning for similar radiance.
Stretching for falling petals
as borrowed clothing
in futile masquerade,
weeping from inferiority,
abounding only in quantity
until weeded, discarded,
grasping roots untangled from shared soil,
cast broken before their long-stemmed gods
in sacrifice,
the garden's fertile earth
reserved for the rose.

Jeaniene Frost

Renewal by the Ocean

This morning,
as I breathed in the pure ocean air
and looked out over the water,
I placed a flesh-colored hibiscus behind my ear.
The pink veins pumped
into a brilliantly colored interior.
Now,
as I step into the ocean waters,
I offer it,
calling out to the goddess Yemaya
as the waves dance around me.
I slowly turn against the sun in
one . . . two . . . three . . .
circles, speaking out the prayer,
purifying body, heart, soul.
Water courses from my hair,
down my breasts, splashes at my feet
as I return to shore.
I am released, free to travel forward,
renewed.

Heysha Marie Diaz

Alive

To she who makes me live

Soaring on wings past midnight
Flying before the moon
Morning star still riding high
Caressed in the darkness
Singing with the breaking dawn
Come day
I shall wing my way above
Climbing the purple clouds
To the vaunted wisps on high
Burn me, thou, oh, sun
Leave no shadow to mark the virgin Earth
Early, revealed before my eyes
I am alive, I am alive
Rejoice, oh, newborn of morning, I am alive

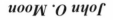

John O. Moon

Artist's Profile
Arshad Ahmed
London, United Kingdom

This poem was written during some of the darker days of my life when I had more questions than answers. I always use music and poetry as an outlet for my feelings. "Explanation by Hatred" is one of them, and I hope you can appreciate it.

Explanation by Hatred

To family and friends

For others, you are the epitome of beauty.
To me, you are a scantily clad abyss
In which one may fall and crawl,
But never leave.

What we see is a possible vision of what we want to be,
But is it a mere reflection
Or an opportunity to sculpt our legacy?

Man will die in vain, a prisoner of his conflict,
While others will weep at their fate.
But none will raise their head in anger and question why.

It is not what we are taught, but what we accept.
Villainy or vice, it's all an explanation by hatred.

Arshad Ahmed

starfish

for sons and lovers

my son's tiny fingers
fat starfish
barely stretch across
the steel strings
of my lover's guitar
the guitar's owner almost left me
because of this son
looked me in the eye
or probably not
and said i cannot do this anymore
oh i have heard these words
from lovers across the world
so i took a deep breath
to make sure none of my ribs
had broken
when my son's tiny fingers
blind starfish
reach a bad note or five
we rewrite
the song of love
again

Vicki Whicker

One Perfect Word
To poets and their poetry

On the sandy gravelly beach
On a large sketch pad
barefoot with a glass of wine
totally alone
And where is that one-legged heron
when I need him to whisper
the message
that one perfect word or phrase
he overheard the wind sending to me

I will not erase
I promise to scratch out and rearrange
with arrows and side notes
and thus I will preserve
the thought processes
and building blocks
intimacy
from inception to conception
for your pleasure
my love
the words I arrange

Mary Hunt

washing up

he would do the dishes
in a linoleum shiny kitchen
(that resonated from years of want
and spilt milk)
with a three-year-old girl
who loved the bubbles
who had started life as an accident
who would turn into a teenager

water pooling lazily on a benchtop was forgotten
a tea towel busying itself absentmindedly in a bowl
hands heavy with age
hiding like chipped china
under the foam
that jump out in occasional tea towel snaps
and identical eyes (two separate, matching sets)
glint like polished glass

life spills out
detergent slick
and foams over a downtrodden floor

leaving a mother in the living room
sipping on silence

Sophia Chapman

Liquid Fun

The fog rolling over my brain
With quickness and severity
Trying to avoid it run from it
Clouding my judgement as I progress
Sending me into oblivion? Reality?
Wanting to hide from something
But do not know what
Only my sea legs to guide me
Can't see anything in front of me
If I crash into it might be my last
A grand explosion the curtain falls
Will it be my last?
No one knows

Jared Sheade

My Father's Red Ruby Orange Tree

In memory of my father, mom and Rubig, my niece, February 2004

After my father's funeral
Walked down in his garden
Wanting to connect to
What he had left behind.
Wildflowers overshadowed
The once cultivated vegetable garden,
New sprouts emerged.
His empty box of cigarettes,
Mixed in the soil, is still there,
Still there, like an empty shell!
I looked yonder,
The red ruby orange tree
Stood bold, high, and free.
Red ruby oranges
Were hanging bright and free,
Washed and drenched by the rain
As if cleansed, ready for the dance.
I grabbed a few red ruby oranges;
The higher the branches, the bigger
And brighter were the oranges.
Soar up high to the light,
Soar up high to the source of light,
Soar up high,
Oh, my father's red ruby orange tree!

Sossy Nercessian

Timeless

Lying under blue skies,
Miles away from home.
Breaking free of ties,
Having our minds roam.

Dreaming endlessly,
Making new plans.
Seeing as far as the eye can see.
Drawing hearts and "I love you's" in the sand.

Driving on winding roads
With no set direction.
Not worrying about what the future holds,
Just knowing there is a connection.

Watching the sun fade under the bed of clouds.
Later counting the stars, while sharing chocolate kisses.
Our bodies wrapped in a golden shroud,
And we decided to make funny faces.

Rolling down golden hills,
Bringing up childhood memories.
Our laughter resonating from the thrills,
Events unfolding into stories.

Nhat Ha Hoang Nguyen

Artist's Profile
Jacqueline Kory
Concord, CA, USA

I am a young poet born in 1989 in Lake Arrowhead, California. I have always enjoyed writing, especially poetry. My parents, Caroline and David, have always supported my writing, and my sisters, Rachel and Katherine, like reading my work. Besides writing, I love to read nearly all genres, from sci-fi novels to historical fiction. I also enjoy the sport of fencing, which evolved from medieval sword fighting. The poem I wrote for this volume was inspired partly by my own feelings, and partly by emotions I merely observed.

Fragile

To friends and family

You.

No words to speak.
Standing silence,
still water ripples . . .
a glance across the room.

Glass shards falling,
carving air like stone . . .
fragile whispers
stirring melted ice.

A single moment . . .
poised between earth and sky.
Our worlds merge. . . .
I am left changed.

Jacqueline Kory

My Prediction

Lying my back on this bed of ice
A bronze leaf flutters down from the sky
A message slipping from the desk of God
Through heavy air and chancing unto me
Yet I ache with reluctance to express
My gratitude that is overshadowed by fear
My judgement is not finalized
I have looked through the windows
Of a certain soul
And wonder upon my depth . . .
In future destiny
My heart genuinely loves. . . .
Why do I predict more rain?

Dayna Elizabeth Lunstrum

crystalline roughs

dew still drawn upon the leaves
woman dressed in silk of light
leads the man from the empty land
groups of travelers peer from woodwork
to hear the wisdom of light unknowing
which way to turn and which sight of light
washes the man's face from the empty land
gestures of the plum from the ground
hold gazes of what is unknown
the empty day and the weeping willow
strolling dreams feel breeze of dawn
twilight fades and armies of swans gather
they stagger to the woman in silk like
empty sand chatters to form rock to come
man from the empty land steals dreams
in the shape of a question pondered from hazed moments

Eric Barbagiovanni

Temporal Spring
To mankind

Words of spring generated
no weight at a glance,
abundance of souls,
and lectures of fragrance.
Heating sparks
of sunsets that color
like horses carrying
imagination that follows.
Temporal spring
being in my mind,
about vain present,
no future to find.
Reality beating,
hard to describe
the use of gold
in a vacuum to try.
Thought by the origin,
hoping cannot find
a way into a soul,
heart as a cry.
Like a growing root,
no steps to be heard,
away from the world,
hides in reverse.

Edgar Escalante

Short Bit of Eternity

It is an ebony embrace
A warm darkness, a calm
Glass ocean endless in
Its reach. It is an old hammock
Ignoring the march of time,
Holding our naked forms,
Swinging gently.

It is an old high school
Friend, her face a bit older
Now that a hard decade
Has slipped on by.
It is her soft breath,
The wisp of her hair
Against my arm.

It's just one moment
Shaking its fist as
It gently sways. It is
All I've ever had.
A short bit of eternity
A drift among a glass ocean,
Endless in its reach.

David Joseph Welch

Artist's Profile
Morgan D. Merithew
Coalinga, CA, USA

This poem came as an onset of studying in my room. Being away from home in college is a different experience. I am so far away that the free dancing spirit within me is lost until the rain releases it. This is for all the free dancing spirits.

The Dancer

She sits in her room
quietly watching the world pass her by.
Gently, she embraces the textbook,
reading about the mystical beauty of the world.
She opens the window
and the wind takes her by surprise.
Its effervescence illuminates the room,
releasing her broken spirit.
The pitter-patter of raindrops
gently dance on the roof.
A slight smile comes to
her delicate face.
Within herself,
she is dancing,
dancing in the rain,
dancing in the textbook,
dancing in her heart.
She sits in her room
quietly watching the world pass her by,
a dancing heart and a rainy window.
She gazes out . . . and sighs.

Morgan D. Merithew

Artist's Profile
Pankaj Mala Bhattacharya
Calcutta, India

I was born and brought up in a small village surrounded by majestic hills situated in northern India. During my childhood, listening to the stories of shepherds and woods was a source of inspiration to me. Later, for education and a job, I moved on to big cities. In the din of busy life, I missed the mountains, which till now spark the little girl in me.

Memories

To my home village

Whilst in Kangra hills
one evening, as I watched from the boat
drifting down the fuzzy stream,
rejuvenation assailed me.
I saw an idle shepherd
leading the herd of woolly sheep;
the woods and meadows they enjoy,
they cry, they uplift their emotions,
they throw about cascades of milieu.
In retrospect; I got a closer look
at life. . . .
I still recall those nights,
those cold, gloomy, sleepless winter nights
sitting by the silvery waterfall
trying to smell the yet unbloomed flowers,
trying to peer across the lofty mountains,
trying to understand life. . . .
Oh! Thou mountains,
I still remember thee,
and I wish
I could there be again.

Pankaj Mala Bhattacharya

Charismatic Patchwork

The waves danced to the music of morning
as the cheekbones of night were tickled by the rising sun.
Alone, she tiptoed near the shore.

Sliding 'neath the charismatic patchwork of aqua and teal
into a valley of sand where dreams are made,
she slept as the echoes of a white-capped lullaby
renewed her soul.

Lydia Shutter

decomposition

strange sounds we made
music
the best parts
being notes unplayed

till our cause
became the pause
between two stanzas of anger

a tainted song
this beat
broken
is a boat
carrying our chords like corpses

we drift off-key to sink

this bond is a bridge
hanging between bars
clawing for distant choruses

we are drums adrift
from the anchor of bass
monotony of verses

Owen Agustus Ellis

Artist's Profile
Alleigh Whitaker
Plymouth, IN, USA

When I write, I write the first thing that comes to mind. It's like I write in random thoughts. I'm not really sure if my surroundings or the people around me inspire me, but this is how my poems turn out. I write what I feel and what I think. Sometimes I don't understand how I come up with some of the things I write, but I really like the outcome of my poems. Maybe one day others, along with myself, will fully understand my feelings through what I have to write.

Unspoken

Broken thoughts
Invisible photographs
Lost in the mind
Streams of tears
Fall down an empty face
Puddles of thoughts form
So tantalizing
Those sleepless nights
From complete stillness
And the forgotten footprints
Of plastic baby dolls
Diagram a quick escape
Visualize the tormenting roller coaster
Bungee jump from the sky
But don't fall
Color a picture of complete happiness
The paper turns out blank
Bruised and broken
Tattered and torn
As all dreams
Shatter

Alleigh Whitaker

Charity

To my sister, Hannah, I love you

Cinnamon pearls of synthetic lullabies
Gently soothing to dreamful state.
Sharing bliss with so few,
A power so strong, brilliant, great.
Fly on wings of purest night,
Timeless beauty stretched so thin.
Six millennia of endless dark
Waiting for obsidian.
Ambrosial red, so shiny and bright,
Elixir of death and flowing light.
Ivory smooth now tinged rosy
Tickles the tongue and expunges the fright.
"Be not wary, my darling,
The night is in your grasp,
Where time and place have no substance
And the tick and tock stop at last."
Ultimate birth from an age-old mother,
Dark and daring, she grasps my hand,
A perfect picture of timely death,
The holy mother, the queen of the damned.

Emily Gregg

Modest Little Tragedy

For Kat, the gypsy

"I'm tired with nothing to say."
I pushed through my teeth
so eroded with fiction.
Everything is sad piano today,
tragic as a painting of a dirty kitchen.

Peering out through jail bar blinds,
these married eyes, dry as the dirt,
ushering in the thin, washed light,
to the sky show soundtrack
of a feathered flirt.

I witnessed decay in digital season,
when the candles cried themselves to death
in a sawdust forest of actions and reasons,
all the snow that peppers the bed.

My bidding for her heart outdone by another.
I could love only now an actress who could play her,
in this room, this tank of low-voltage color
stained a filthy blonde, like ancient paper.

Pup Anitn

Artist's Profile
P. Martin
London, United Kingdom

I am a physically challenged single mother. I am getting on happily with my life and, as usual, I am taking care of both my son's business and my own. This poem is basically about my traumatic experience of marriage, domestic violence, and rediscovery.

Times of Yore
To life and all its adversities

Bad love is
Turmoil making its entrance
With effortless fury
The stale scent of loneliness slinking
Its bitter cape upon my sagging shoulders
Whilst time, patient time, simply loiters on
Bad love, along with a bloody nose
Is an habitual tablespoonful of contempt
Stagnant emotions
Vulnerability
And all that psychological abrasion
Whilst time, malicious time, simply loiters on
The submissive disciple, too long in a deep slumber
But long before discontent reigned
And insecurity gnawed
Good love was strolls down Amen Street Market,
Saunas on Sunday afternoons
Listening to Coltrane
Good love was
A two-ounce tub of Italian ice cream
Warm evenings conversing
Over chilled bottles of white wine,
Soft music, and origami

P. Martin

Untitled

May the eyes of truth
Always pierce your heart
Refracting like an ancient prism
Reflecting the beauty of your soul
Sacred mirror with shimmering visions
Lives once lived and those yet to be born
May wind and water inspire you
Offering their vessels from far away
Gaze upon them with wonder and hope
Draw from them strength to create
May moonbathed velvet nights
Intoxicate you with sensual promise
May your warm whisper of song
Always tickle sweet flesh
May eyes soft and deep
Always tell what you feel inside
Swaying in the cradle of connection
Soaring with the four winds
Blessed
Alive
Eternal

Megan Sullivan

On Stage

She has an arched poise,
sharp eyes that lock
every fragment of her seeing vision.
Her pale cream voile dress
is just to elude the blind
audience from her svelte rebuke.
No one dares to approach her
dignified Athena stature,
afraid to confront the
truth in her eyes,
exposing their illusions of
comfort and ego.
It's the split wood
scent of hard drinks
in which they can
melt into anti-reality.
On stage she speaks
in kind care at this
destruction of joy
and human will,
and inside she burns
with grave disgust.

Michelle Xiao

In Reference to an Earthworm
To someone

It's androgynous!
screamed the boy with lights
dancing in his eyes
watching the sun laugh and play
in her hair
while she captured him
with her tiger trap eyes
in reference to an earthworm.
It squiggled and squealed with silent
throes of attempted escape
coursing through its slimy frame
in the boy's fingers
holding with firm gentleness
of a spider's deathly grasp
sun shining off its shiny length
yearning for earth's moisture.
Flying above with wind
she juggled clouds under wing
wanting worms to eat
bird spirits rising
she swooped
and dropped
and grabbed the worm
to the screams of young girl.

Reyad Williams

Educated Fall

In memory of my mother's father

My grandpa stands behind me on the pier.
Before we go he wants to see me dive,
to make use of the pink towel shroud
about his hips. When we leave here,
I will have split the sea with my fingertips.

I cannot look as I raise my arms above my head
and press my palms in silent prayer,
wishing that somehow I would not be bed
into the stony bottom with the sunken ships . . .
and then his hand presses upon my spine,
the blood rushing to my head as I try to save
a glacial breath, until I taste the salt that splits my lips.

This is how I fall, lungs swollen with ocean,
then heaving upon the planks, warm against my skin.

Matthew S. Cohen

The Branch

Water rushes quickly past,
but I move not an inch.
My damp skin shivers in the coolness about.
but still I hold my place.
Eddies and riffles all around
soft wake at my edges.
The world happens all around me,
but stillness is my only reaction.
Wind blows softly rustling leaves,
still I stay immobile.
The hard edge I rest upon
bars my movement,
and blocks my path in the flow of life.

Paul Branly

urban nights

a cold wind blows
past the blackened snow
and a car sends
slush to the curbside
reflecting in the streetlight
is a fall from grace
with red neon lights
seen through the fog and haze
sitting stagnant in the sky
as the city throbs
to the heartbeat
of the nightclub
pumping life
to the night wanderers
alone amidst the crowd
unsure of the future
unsure of its meaning
and the earth
sends its tears
watering the withering
eggplants on the windowsill

Cortney Creswick

Artist's Profile
David C. Wenger-Keller
Fort Madison, IA, USA

I am fifty-two years old. I live in a small town in Iowa where I work hard as a physician, cook, read murder mysteries, tend a small garden, and write poems. My favorite poets are Nikki Giovanni, e. e. cummings, Charles Bukowski, and Billy Collins.

One Rightful Hand

Without you
I am abstract-able,
unbearable,
like a lime-greed orchid shirt
over pants with
wide orange vertical stripes.
I can no more resist this
passion for you
than a kitchen sieve
can resist the ocean.
When we are together,
your magic is luxurious,
graceful,
and certain to make me smile.
Ours is a malicious ecstasy,
a desolate passion,
an irresistible rectitude,
and one rightful hand
on the sword in the stone.

David C. Wenger-Keller

Artist's Profile
E. Thomas West

Arcata, CA, USA

I am a graduate student searching and finding some transition here, somewhere in the middle of my life. This poem was written as a reminder to me of all the glorious and tumultuous days shared with my graduate school cohort. Each and every one is an inspiration. I love you all. Thank you, and God bless.

Chasing Butterflies on a Windy Day

To my graduate student cohort (you know who you are)

Oh, thoughts and memories cherished
Of challenges and deeds interwoven
With tears and laughter, leapfrogging
Over heart and soul, so innocent . . .
They fill my cup to overflowing.
Oh, sweet nostalgia, remembrance blessed,
You come to me, and with unspoken promises, go
Flitting away upon mischievous wings,
Leaving bittersweet gales, ripping . . .
Through my unsuspecting consciousness.
Oh, joyfully mourn I these enduring, fleeting
Images of glee and suffering past, and yet
Wherefore shall I capture them, so elusive?
In agonized, desperate reaching, I grasp, so much like . . .
Chasing butterflies on a windy day.

E. Thomas West

Quickly She Turned Away

There she stood by the door poised in
Her exciting and provocative attire as
She looked the other way outsmarted by
The thugs watching some people walk
Upon their own business in the golden

Capitalist market when in instantaneous
Moment this girl turned her subtle eyes
My way her eyes were green casting the
Illusion of a love for a moment she was
Mine when quickly she turned away as

She walked away from my heart could
Hear the trade winds whispery through
The palm trees on a private beach with
A mercenary trident at the surface of the
Arcane don't forget about the wire since

It started a fire with all of the patterns of
The skirmishes that the world endures a
Shiny bright diamond bracelet that she
Wears here comes the other girl shiny
Diamonds too dreaming of another girl

G. F. Pettersson

Transit/Prodigal Sun

The sun fell out of a hole in the sky
and rolled down the mountainside
leaving opaline snail trails
on rough gray rocks.

The sun rolled down the mountainside
and across the field
sparking crystal fires
on dew-flecked grass.

The sun rolled across the field
and into the lake
glowing silvery bright
in the watery mirror.

The sun rolled into the lake
and onto the shore
through pearlescent lilies
and pale gold reeds

and into a hole in the sky.

Margery Hauser

Doves

White puffs of smoke smear across the sky,
Moving so passionately with nothing but spry
Everything slows down in a slow moving pace
And you can feel the exquisite embrace
One by one they fill the empty violin bows,
A second of freedom; a second of peace
It's more wealth than a golden fleece
One by one they plunge through the sea
And all their fears are set free
The eye shadow is painted but not on eyes
And leaves a feeling of immense surprise
This is picture perfect, nothing but real
But it's only something that is surreal
Something that can be pictured but not erased
The sky is scarred and has been embraced

Amanda Dixon

Reflection

To fine-feathered creatures who may be their own worst enemies

Among the treetops of his old domain
the raven sees a stranger, menacing
and fearless, of his own kind, handsome, black,
but arrogant, intrusive, out of place,
in need of putting down and sending off.
Rat-tatting on the windowpane, he hopes
to scare the self he does not recognize
into submission and retreat. (The room
behind the window was not there last spring,
the house built while the birds were far away.)
The stranger holds his ground, meets eye with eye,
gives blow for blow, bows when he bows, and when
he stretches for a dominating height
from which to glower down, the stranger looms
no lower, holding undimmed eye to eye.
He has not won but is not beaten yet. He struts
aside to fly to some inviolate place,
returns at dawn to face the taunting other ness
again—and finds it gone (for in the night
a drape whose folds now fog reflection has been hung
behind the pane). His raucous voice is raised to claim
all challengers dispatched . . . too loud, too proud to hear
his only enemy, the echo in the glass
who chuckles softly somewhere deep behind his eyes.

John Bayly

Artist's Profile

Sarah R. Boesger

Elyria, OH, USA

This is a fast poem, written for a fast person. I dedicate this to my best friend, Steven, whose friendship makes the word obsolete. He makes my world more colorful and interesting every day. I thank him for his place in my life.

Green Apple Bellyache
To Steven

You're like a green apple bellyache,
sour and recurring,
never forever
and yet sometimes you're a magnolia
radiant and fresher than a new day

Today I think you're an egg sandwich,
too familiar for my own good
a desire associated with the past
filling me up with your yolky thoughts

Tomorrow I pray for a new day
maybe sour, possibly sweet too,
but always with my green apple bellyache
reminding me of beauty and substance

Sarah R. Boesger

Artist's Profile

Lindsey Parker

Port Coquitlam, BC, Canada

This is one of few poems I've written that I can honestly say I take pride in. It captures the sense of despair I feel when I look around and realize I'm alone. It recollects a time when I didn't feel this way, when even the worst situations weren't completely hopeless. It is written with a particular person in mind and soul, a person I think of every day.

The Light Switch
To my light keeper

She sits silent in a rocking chair
Mindlessly playing with a strand of hair
Wondering how she wound up there

This wasn't what he'd sold to her
No, this was so much colder
This was far too cold to bear

Promises of an eternal sun
In that moment came undone
When her dawn had just begun

The light flickered, then went black
She couldn't make the light come back
She couldn't even see to run

Now she sits in shadows cold
Remembering what she was told
Left with nothing to behold

Before in darkness there were stars
Specks of light that healed her scars
Now just blackness, stale and old

Lindsey Parker

Forty Winks

As I sit here, tossing and turning
I wait here, my cigarette is burning
I've been through this too many times
I'll just be back here, writing emotional rhymes
With unwavering devotion, I persist
just thinking of reasons of why you resist
I'm setting myself up for this
because I know it will only take one kiss
It's like somehow you're laced
because all it takes is just one taste
I can think of a past embrace
and the thought will make my heart race
It's like I'm on a tower taking a dive
I fall, closing my eyes, waiting for the pain to arrive

Jonas Ashbaugh

The Summons
To Round Pond, Maine

With a roar, the life had awakened her.
A northeast wind storm had swept up the channel
And speedily whistled alluringly to her.
It brought to her mind the tang of the salt wastes
And sweet yearning filled her heart to the core.
She imagined the star of the lighthouse
And the blaze of the sunset in the harbor,
All this from hearing the summons of the wind.
Her soul broke loose like a wave of the harbor.
There was a wild fire in her sultry gray eyes.
All her relatives were across the harbor.
She must go at once to be with family.
Despite knowing every inch of the harbor,
She fought the dark and struggled to the boathouse.
She didn't hear the bells across the harbor,
The wind was rising, coming in suddenly.
Up-curling waves pushed against her schooner.
Her knowledge couldn't fight through the raging crests.
She had forgotten the reckless gusty harbor
As saltwater descended upon her face
And the furious wind gusts sprang over her.
For her, a dull, murky sunrise had risen,
At noon the bells were ringing to honor her
Mournfully at a church across the harbor.

Br. James A. Locke

Scarecrows

Each of us on our own ground,
tied to poles,
flapping arms at circling crows,
are waiting.

For we have heard a story
passed from field to field
that when the green stalks grey
and the tassels silver,

poles and ropes will fall away,
and we shall be summoned
by cold winds and fiddling
to dance at the harvest.

John Bing

head above water

the toilet tissue on her shoe
was not the first thing you'd notice.
maybe it would be the lipstick smudges or the salt
from her tuesday afternoon pretzel.
maybe it would be the weight of routine
like writing something too repetitive . . . too pedestrian
to be a poem.
she's late for work again. they pay her.
last year she paid, but never attended;
sat and listened but never really heard.
but last year was
just that. . . .
next year will be different.
she knows it.

Ajah Hales

Crisp Hundred Dollar Bills

Tuxedos and their wearers are new hundred dollar bills.
In various ways they are the same,
Both are crisp and perfect,
Wrinkle-free and smooth,
Both are fresh and clean.

New bills stick together.
Tuxedo wearers clump together in clusters.
Uncomfortable all dressed up,
In a group they hang out together.

New, clean bills are hard to separate.
They need to be peeled apart carefully.
Tuxedo wearers need to be pulled away
From their friends and fellow sufferers.

Jessica Stalker

Fettered

I trace the silvery tracks
On my cheeks . . .
The path of all the tears
I have cried;
The saltwater buildup
Of so many weeks,
The proof of my sad lack
Of pride.
And it's something I wish
That they'd never seen,
A pain I wish
I could just hide.
But it's not a secret,
It never has been,
No matter just how hard
I've tried.
And they will not ignore it
And I'll never forget,
Even after the last tear
Has dried.
Nonchalance is a guise
That I haven't learnt yet;
I will never take this
In my stride.

Jodi Kicinski

The Anatomy of Perception

Infinite nights
Dictated by moonlight.
As minutes gather
Form together and mesh
Gaining momentum
Until perception is lost.
Then all at once,
Time stands still,
Allowing
For the time forgotten
To be re-compensated,
Reclaimed,
And remembered.
As snippets
Of sepia
And black and white
Are to recount
Insignificant moments
Captured from memories
That are all together
Lost,
Jumbled,
And confused.

Brandon David Peterson

Moments Before the Wake

Clear gazes from the polished womb,
all that came in contact swallowed
deep breaths to sulk in the mire of
Sunday's swamp. A partition
separated her children from a world
of indulging in the outer spaces;
snapping their fingers to foreign
beats caring about the other ones,
smacking their lips to the notes.
Some folks seemed to moan after
the rancid memories of days previous
soaked deep into their crispy
pores. As a sun that descended
without remorse, the bearers of its
ray prayed for better and cooler
days, to partake in sleeps that the
gods would envy. Infinite
slumbers were granted throughout the
salted tombs; listening on
the other side of a dense wall were
the children with bare hands
and pink cheeks.

Dustin Davenport

The Music of the Night

The sun vanishes across the horizon,
And a new world has begun,
A world of total darkness
When the day is finally done.
In the black stillness
On a warm summer's night,
Tiny creatures come to life
In the absence of light.
An orchestra then begins to play
Of crickets chirping pleasantly away.
The audience around their music enthralls
As their loud, cheerful melody rises and falls.
Blending with each other,
A lonesome toad joins in.
Its bass-like croak one of a kind,
Though the fiddlers seem not to mind.
Their playing complimenting one another,
A drumbeat holding them all together,
Melodious tunes in harmony,
Enhancing the beauty
Of Mother Nature's symphony.

Felicia Tan Yean Sze

Dust of Stars

Innumerable diamonds light the night.
The clouds have abandoned the sky.
Incredibly beautiful and awesome the universe
As my boat appears to fly.
On the gossamer wings of her sails set full
On this path lit by star shine,
Her wake bubbles effervescent,
Making trails of its own design.
Perhaps the denizens of urban deep
Where streetlights smother the stars,
Should sometimes seek a place like this
Far from the city's scars.
'Tis here they can reflect on life
How insignificant it would be,
If not for God's hereafter
And His love for you and me.
Meanwhile, my ship and I do lie
On this blanket on Heaven's floor
Just breathing in the dust of stars
That swirl from Heaven's door.

Roger Arthur Marin

Artist's Profile
Dawn Hull
Shoreline, WA, USA

This poem is about the energy that is in every living thing. Energy is the basis of everything we do. The fact that energy flows through everything is the one thing that keeps all people and the Earth connected.

soldier of energy
To Mother Earth

static spirals
down dragonfly wings
over
reeds singing wind-
ridden,
like larks lingering
on stream banks,
tornadoes of fluttering
butterflies
up weathervanes
dancing down jagged
barbed wire fences
jaunting towards fields
of rolling lupine,
revolving into
fingertips of velvet
singers' voices,
across plains of faceless
foreheads,
to the apex of everything that is

Dawn Hull

Departure

The lingering night of your departure
wraps its cold body around
the warm chair you occupied,
extending its limp arms tightly around us.

Entwined in your lifeless embrace,
we breathe the fresh aroma
of a caffeine-induced morning,
clutching sun-drenched remnants
of your last visit.

Unearthed treasures float
on the surface of our liquid sorrows
and prove to us that why you left
matters less than why you came.

Gail Levitt

Untitled

To those for whom
the world is a crashing wave
that washes over a raw spirit
singing and stinging
in its salty tongue,
I say find someone.

Not an advocate
or a complement,
but another creature altogether.
Sea-sister, pendant
whose heart-shaped box is the same shape as yours
and holds just as much,
whose swimming soul turns a mirror to your own
and is not afraid
of what it sees.

Now cling to her with all your might.
Whisper in the delicate, pink shell of her ear
your fears of the deep;
listen to the sea wash of her breath.
Float face up in the dark
and together search the sky
for answers.

Miranda Whitmore

When Water Falls Like Rocks

As the night gave birth
To a fruitless sky
The windows blew open
And feathered wings carried me away.
Higher and higher they flew
Until they finally released.
I fell as the wind ripped
Every error from my spotless soul.
I was high on freedom
'Til at last I hit the water
Where I was swept away
And my mind was blown elsewhere.
It didn't matter, though, because today
I had led the pack and set the direction.
They'll never catch me now.
My water outdid your steel
Centuries ago.
No one thought I'd get this far
And they won't know 'til tomorrow
When they find the picture incomplete
And a window leading to a day
That I've already seen.

Amy F. Goggin

the flood

cool pale night full moon
lightning screams across the sky
tears into my heart
open water gushing flows
through the cracks in the stone wall

yielding rains pour down
gently washing over me
part my lips look up
swallowing as if to speak
the drops silently urge on

what life i see peeks
from beneath the fallow ground
one tiny speck moves
to call forth a warm west wind
it sleeps and waits for daybreak

lush wet blades of grass
move beneath my feet stepping
over fallen leaves
feeling the earth now running
joy flits on butterflies' wings

Adrienne Duryee

uncouth cogitation

the words faintly go adrift
and prance before the moon
the gawking grass then looks up
and starts belting out a tune
the brush-stroked sky
then falls to the sea
and the smoke doth form a rift
as underneath the willow tree
light transforms some fancy gifts
then the prancing words look up
to see what had arrived
and bursting images and colors
then shatter through your eyes
blinding you from what is real
and mingling on the grass
then they sink in gently
with everything from the past
sometimes this is where you go
when nestled in your dreams
out on the grassy knoll of blue
nothing is quite what it had seemed

Jessica Berube

The Study of Self-Portrait

"I'd misrecognize me anywhere" - Stan Regal

I look like someone
yet no one
but otherwise resemble some echo
you've never heard of.
Caught up in mad pursuit
across experience and reappearance
of pinned butterflies' wings
on the back of the mountain
I have recklessly forsaken
the nuptial vows
for everywhere.
In the lethargy of goof
the irrational vision of
feathered high peaks
rolling over silly fault plains
and indifferent fields
reveal that I'm lost
in incandescent brightness.
Eager to hear shepherds converse
I'm somewhere closer to politicians
nowhere near angels.

Rosa Arlotto

Maggie Thatcher's Election

Slept on a park bench last night,
The cold warmth of Maggie Thatcher
Wrapped around my body.
The evening paper smells of chips,
My stomach grinds and slips,
Salivating again.
I awake to a social order,
Geese fly in spirals above my head.
I asked for some money today
From a man who smelled of death.
I could taste it on my breath
Long after he walked away.
These days there are reapers in the
Crowd.
And the sun refuses
To play.

Barb J. Trglavcnik

Shiver
For my son

The afternoon sun shimmers on the gum trees
A gentle wind blows
Their leaves shiver and dance
Oh, what a lovely sight
You can almost feel their delight
The gums shiver at me with a twinkle in their leaves
Branches sway in harmony with the soft cool breeze
How lovely and peaceful they stand
So tall and grand
Singing to themselves and me
Their bark glows white
In the twilight
As the sun goes low
Their age begins to show
Leisurely the zephyr retreats
The gum trees become still
The inky softness of dusk descends
The moon creeps over the hill
Throwing tranquil shadows over the gums
That are now barely visible
Nightfall has silenced their performance
Yet the gums still shiver to me

Ursula M. Hoy

Artist's Profile
Peter T. Monacelli
Brockport, NY, USA

To me, poetry is about capturing a moment in time forever. It becomes a gift to the reader when he or she chooses to embrace, identify and internalize it without limits. My verses are written with the intent to draw the reader into my mind and look through my eyes for a moment. It is my hope that through these experiences, people will stop from time to time and attempt to view the world as I see it.

Watercolors in Shades of Gray

Memories of the lake in winter
Like watercolors in shades of gray
The wind cascades over the hill
While snowflakes dance in the sky
In the distance a fog-like cover
Envelops the ominous horizon
A misty airy feeling arises slowly
As the trees sleep in a blanket of snow
Fungus steps emerge from the old willow
As a secret wonderland unfolds
If you listen closely the fairies giggle
While they spread their magic dust
Water rushes down the hillside
Trickling over stones worn smooth
Enchanted music plays on the headset
My soul is at peace in this place
Metaphoric cracks run deep within the walls
Transcending surreal awakenings in my mind
Memories such as these shall remain forever
Blending like watercolors in shades of gray

Peter T. Monacelli

In Your Face

Northern pike
lurking in green, spotted weed,
back-pointing teeth
search for bluegill
at the edge of deep water
A dart, quick snap
swallow headfirst,
mistaken bait
Sucker completely soaked,
bobber sinks
luring the boat to a tippy angle
A fish tale born
A sudden tug,
tension
pulling and bending whiz of line
A surface tease splashes in your face
A final tail kick
flashes the hammer handle
back into the depths
in the world of lake
quiet . . . smooth bottom
a swirl into the darkness

Jennifer Lintelmann

The Burning of the Roses

The burning of the roses red
Oh fair young flowers fallen dead
Gray ashes of a blossom head
A resting place from flowerbed

Sweet peaceful broken lily heart
Of hope and dreams now torn apart
A graceful awe of earthen art
Oh life that naught but had a start

Pure innocence and doorless pain
Dear daffodil its roots a chain
Trapped helpless doomed to burn in vain
Oh children's laughter silent slain

Gazed yonder eyes whom you were chose
Saw none behind the dark windows
Soft drums of secret haunting woes
Of lost love and your ashen rose

Erika Craig

Message Among the Waves

In memory of W. B. Yeats, an inspiration

Gaze turns to pondering sea;
Waves of turquoise ever lapping.
An army of ranks swirling strong
As they crash upon soft shore.
Their beating drums are timeless,
Filling both ear and mind.
Recalling memories of old
Without regret or care.
Somber, they move forward
Rolling with rough white crest.
Beautiful, yet dangerous, they call. . . .
I listen to their sad song.
The sand beneath weary feet
Is white and worn so soft.
The fine grains gathering
Over many centuries now lost.
Each grain, although small
And insignificant alone,
Does have a story of its own.
All I do is listen. . . .
Like words strewn across nature's page
Do they flow in endless lines.
It is left for us alone to discover
The message among the waves.

Jennifer Wardle

Rising from Smoke

When the hollowed chords in my lungs
constrict my ribs, my spine,
do I have a jog or a cigarette?
The answer is thicker than blood.

When anonymous, he wraps arms 'round
my veins to pulse downward,
do I give a shove or a sigh?
The answer is crumbling granite.

The caterpillars think I'm a tree.
They push and pull their fuzzy neon
on the back of my neck, tickling.
By accident, or not,
I did not,
and returned the squishy tube
intact
to a half-eaten leaf.

Stacey Wrona

collapse
To my mom

another grey hair contrasting youth
the root of it in his soul
a scar there left too long covered
a past wound, but he's not too sure how it came to be
only that she said
the wound would give him pain
and courage
"a bandage to fix all this blood?"
he asked
but she only smiled, and shattered
sighing
how fragile we are
he collected the pieces in a box
sat it over his fireplace
and became a hard man, made a name
"the key to life," he said, " is to
avoid memories and carve a spartan face in this game of
ruthless belligerents"
and then the wound bleeds more,
staining his crisp white shirt
he sits dying and asks himself
"am i waking up slowly?"

Cori Todoroff

Light

A thousand points of light,
like a thousand dreams in the sea.
They bounce the waves,
sometimes defy the waves;
my daughter likes the twinkling water.

To capture this moment would be ideal, but somehow I feel as if I
am being captured, photographed by thousands of angels.
My every expression, each passion,
is captured, saved.
In faith there is hope, and my dreams are in the sea.

Lisa M. Jones

To Build in Concave

A little broken myrtle
that spilt at your door,
and filled your halls and rooms
with customs that appealed to your scent.

A plateau of divine and devout
who bent at your heels
and convinced their provider of light
that they were here to serve.

A custom that keeled at riches
and peeled its way
off the plaster you worked to supply.

A kinder remark
for the twigs you gathered to be built.
We see that it may pucker up.
So we build it in concave
and hope this will clasp the fall.

Claudette Visco

She Is

She is the sweet smell
of disintegration,
blending in a salty fog,
particles diffused
into the essential.
She is a darkness that bates
suicide over
the undulating sea.
She is the promised calm that
begs emptiness in
an ebony shrill deep,
leading to stillness,
far from this moment,
nearing defection.

Y. D. Sotelo

Influences

Pathways of fate narrowed by choices
Send you away and then back to the self
A glimpse in a book from a dusty shelf
Thoughts of love lost by helpless forces

Crossroads of life relative in perceptions
Call you afar and then drive you to hope
A spark of perfection in a physical world
Feelings of lust found by true deceptions

Corridors of love implanted in awareness
Reach you inside and then outside they die
A moment of delight lost in a worldly lie
Expressions of life in hourglass unfairness

Timelines of hope from parallel spaces
Sway you silent and then loudly attack
A piece of the puzzle is given back
Unification of energy in existences

Victor Rosca

Consequence

I sat in speckled shadows,
Litter on the ground and whispers in the air.
Amongst broken shards of glass,
Insects would breed in the cracked pavement.
Tree leaves coasted on the wind,
Clawing at the ground.
The rain pulled itself from the soil,
Launching into space.
Trees crumbled and collapsed,
Fading into dust.
The oceans opened up,
Swallowing themselves.
The moon abandoned us
As stars were erased from the sky.
No light from up above,
The clouds decomposed.
The blackness of the night seemed to fade
Until the sky didn't exist.
And then there was nothing.
I held my head with dirty hands
As I sat in speckled shadows.

Christy Gigante

Harvey
To Nadine

So drag me under,
as your intent reigns
beneath the dark skies,
angels cry tears
to know hate
the way you seem to.
Belief is far beyond;
no returning to who
or how it once was.
Demeaning stares;
the knowledge of right and wrong,
and the inability of conscientious decision.
Stolid eyes reveal nothing,
for there is no future
in knowing the past.
Distinctly sagacious in nature,
although no one would begin
to predict it.
Who's to tell
the moral authenticity
of the situation at hand,
when the answer desired
is inconceivable
to the victims.

Andrea Harvey

Post-Popular Music

Although refreshing
it was,
I was caught in cold sweats,
shivering in the airless spaces
of the city
after dark, during artificial
light time.

She was laughing,
I guess.
So was I,
but not at him
in the ragged, plastic bag clothing
and the swollen eyelids.
The duality of my emotions,
nervous sickness,
was more amusing.

Shaking
for me, she was of another
time and he,
bludgeoned chin,
was
another place entirely.

Jannika Emilia Hildén

Weather

Personified trees ached as the wind bent
Them strongly, giving their boughs a moan.
The forest in its peace held me, continued.

Those leaves above and the shrubs below
Created and built, then grew and slept;
In the fall they slept, their leaves below.

A deer (an adult) pressed quickly to hide,
And I listened (thinking on impermanence,
Then on a girl and then her permanence).

The clearing held my car and the air
Tasted different than the autumn forest;
The sound of the road and the run of air.

Brian Gatz

Departing . . . A Leaf's Tale

I hurried out today as any day, to
See the things I saw yesterday.
I took shortest shortcut, but tree
Stands in my perfect geometry.

Banana skin
Is shifting ground, swinging cloud,
And slows me
Down by your root,

But tree season is having its regret.
Sky blue washes through your golden net.
Then one departing leaf is sailing with the wind,
And the butterfly is waltzing after her twin;
A thousand leaves are clapping hands,
Cherishing their brother's finishing dance.

Night, I recollect the leaf's pleasure
While preparing for tomorrow's early departure.

Wei Li

Building

The house I grew up in was built of straight lines,
right angles, and smooth, solid walls
to divide inside from outside,
a mat to wipe off the earth's mud
and windows to survey the state of the world.
All solid, the architect unquestioned.
But you and I are building now
and it is ours to decide these things,
to move this wall over there
and that here, there will not be a wall . . .
instead, a large window for watching the rain
and another in the washroom,
where we'll wave merrily to the neighbors from the bathtub.
There will be soft rugs on wooden floors,
flickering candles on walls, and a fireplace simmering in warmth
with rich, woody smoke escaping through cracks,
melting the outside snow.
It will be ours and we are in love with building
but walking through the hallways some days
through these rooms without doors,
I feel the older builders watching us
and hesitate, afraid for a moment
to look back and find it
made only of toothpicks and marshmallows.

Darla Rehorst

Sophie

Sophie sits on a wooden floor of
honey, crossed legs, pressed palms,
pale complexion and delicate hair.
She smells of the cold winter behind
her. The anger in her eyes bangs
against mine as if a door slammed by
a sudden change of mind. Her
attempted smile has scattered
freckles on faintly panted cheeks; an
effort to look alive. Outside the
photograph, Sophie walks alone. Snow
drips down from somewhere no one has
ever seen. In a store window Sophie
and her reflection are perfect and
flawed, pure and stained. The glass
sweats with fog and Sophie whispers
incoherent words and writes
"violate" in her steamy breath
with her own dirty finger.

Rebecca Powers

The Conversation

He lay warm in the high, wide bed, listening
to the comfortable voices lapping gently
against the closed door. Familiar forms loomed
indistinctly in the crack of light. The wing-chair
at an angle by the south-facing window, where
next week, or the following, he would watch
the flowers breaking from the bulbs' green bills,
and the children, satchels bumping, playing tag
on the way to school. The old, dark, oval frames.
Indecipherable, his mother with her piled hair,
seated. Indecipherable, his father's proud,
proprietary hand poised on her shoulder.
The schoolhouse above the lake. Deirdre
smiling from the chest of drawers she chose
that still contained folded in tissue with
a lavender bag, her frilly things, her few bits
of jewelry, letters, and her wedding veil.
The dress long since cut down for christenings.
"You're sure?" "It's for the best. He needs
full-time attention, and I thought the matron
kind and efficient. The room is very pleasant, and
the company will do him good. Take him
out of himself." "Come on, let's go to bed."
Beneath the unseen door, the lights went out.

Lorna Rusbridge

The Bearded Man
For my mother

The hurting bearded man
Rubs the soreness from my shoulders.
Two bowls of pitch
From under cocoa butter folds
Shake me to my core
And learn all of my secrets.
The hateful bearded man
Wraps around me like a sheet.
Two patches of spring sky
From under the sharp folds
Fill me with clarity and with calm.
The heavy bearded man
Drenches me like rain.
Two saucers of vast green ocean
From under the frightened folds
Beg me for approval,
And hands to carry the burden.

Emily Upham

The Birth of Autumn

Pregnant gray sky gave birth
To a flock of black birds.
The gray split in two,
And stray shatters of glass
Falling down cut open
The autumn cocoon.
It unfolded its wings
And heavily flew down and
Got meshed in the wires of the city.
It rained all life long
And only the satin sleeping
On the shoulders of beautiful women
Dreamt of summer
And ripe purple cherries.

Nonna Turusbekova

No Correlation
To my late grandparents

The last thing my grandfather ate
before he died was a tomato.
He sat down in the dining room,
placed the plump orb on top of
the cutting board and sliced
through it with a sharp, thin knife
until he reached the familiar woody sturdiness
that the table, the chairs, and the house
all shared, supporters of human instability.
As he slid the thick red slabs into his mouth,
he glanced out the window
and saw a deer pestering his garden.
He rose from his seat to attend to this disturbance,
but as he stood, his legs folded under him
and his mind went to sleep.
My grandfather crumpled to the floor
and, like the knife, came to rest
on the same familiar sturdiness
that had borne him for so many years.

Guy McClellan

Artist's Profile

Norah Lyonhill-Smith
Boonville, NC, USA

In literature throughout the ages, young men have been beset with a burning desire for older women. In this poem, we look in upon a beautiful Victorian woman and her young, now grown to manhood, adoring, would-be beau. The invitation has been given and a lengthy dance of seduction is brought to a close as the lovers come to together within the lilacs' fragrant, hidden sanctuary.

The Lilac

To lovers everywhere

Come sit beneath the lilac shade,
breathe by me much bolder
A year has passed since summer's last,
both you, and I, are older
Come sit beneath the purple spray,
tell me of your growing
How just beyond your tender years
you come to reap the knowing
You stand quite tall now, I do mark,
your eyes, they vie my own
And there upon your once-smooth cheek
a caste of mettle has grown
Underneath the fragrant bower
this evening we'll recline
You may tell me of your yearnings
while I seek and gather mine
You burn me with your gaze young man,
purporting your intent
The innocence of last year's spring,
I do ponder where it went
Embrace me with your weight, sweet boy,
cover sin's joy over
Below the lilacs' dense bloom
our passion melts the clove

Norah Lyonhill-Smith

Everywhere and Nowhere at the Same Time

I'm sitting with
My grandmother
Among things

That don't belong to
Either of us
She kisses my hand

Gently, like lapping
Waves against sandy shores
She whispers

Goodbye, goodbye
Until we dance
This dance again

Mary O'Neill

Lamentation

As the sun falls into irrevocable slumber,
gargoyles: we breathe behind stone,
encasing bleeding hearts
not untouched by what we pretend to be,
but somehow removed
so that . . . in blossom,
innocence resurrected,
we become children, you and I.
And I know you . . . somehow.
I think I had spoken your name once,
but it had been long ago.
Long before we remember.
But . . . as subtle as a stray summer breeze
swallowed by winter's betraying tidal,
I can recall something
hidden in your eyes.
I'd like to think that
things will never change,
but they always manage to
anyway.

Jessica Pollman

My Hill

I am the lion
basking in my endless glory as I survey my pride land.
The safari of weeds envelops me into
a mix of eye-popping yellows and swampy greens.
I journey farther.
The sickly sweet smell of cherry blossoms
slowly parades around me
and then hangs low in a thick haze.
Two petite ivory white butterflies
dance delightedly in a flawless duo
but are they really dancing?
What if it is like a car accident to them
and all we see is them bickering?
They separate
off to call their insurance company.
A smile slinks casually upon my face and
the worries of my adolescent life melt away
as the sun melts away into
the horizon.

Sarah Beaty

Damp Collections

People want to hear
about deadened leaves
draping a cobblestone road,
about the ferocity of wind
and the unexplainable
calmness it brings once
the crisp, cool air is inhaled,
allowing the stillness
to reside within
the meat of minds,
freeing limbs from
their roots buried deep
in a damp collection
of white lies and guilt.

People want to confess
dreams and fears,
doubts that eat the
stomach's inner lining.
Except there are no words,
only lonely glances.

Nancy Silva

on returning

on returning
pictures in my mind
convey her
to be free she says
to be clad in
passion

on returning
she glides across
pages of want
of solitude
and yearning

on returning
i see her
feel her press
against me
with her hands
upon my face

on returning
i find her blind

Jacques Smit

Your Memory

Your image was a contour on my atlas,
Holding your throbbing reminiscence in the cracks of my mind,
And with vigor I rubbed till there was only a smudge,
With the stubborn resolve to forget.
But your smudge remains more stubborn,
As prominent as valleys and peaks on the scale,
Blocking road symbols with its silent illustration,
Which the waves of the Pacific won't wash.
And the motive not to reflect,
Twists and squirms in your reflection,
And though your eyes shall flicker no more,
I see them open against my verdict.
In speech or in dialect our senses mirrored,
Akin to the sea and sky where blue divides,
I knew the lines of your skin and the shades in your conviction,
But a logical path I cannot find.
However, if I sit solidly here with the ticking of time a blur
And let emotion take me back to our sacred tie
I shall become a callow stream with obstructions at every turn,
And I shall fade.
No other shall venture into my contemplation,
With the equal empathy as your expression verified,
Now my sentiment shall emulate in tears alone as death looks on.

Melissa Smith

classroom

neon inside
outside afternoon
and ferns
behind the glass
where the wind is

blackboard chalk words
chart illusions
square chairs make square bodies
and the sun is round

but neon flickers so fast
you don't see the break in the line
and fall into lino speckles
or the color of your sweater
while grey sun trees are hissing

Helga Weiss